THIS
ENGLAND
JOB

W0007291

by Stan Liversedge

Also by the author

Liverpool Football Club
The Official Liverpool FC Centenary Book
Liverpool From The Inside
Forever Everton!
Big Jack: The Life and Times of Jack Charlton
Busby: Epitaph to a Legend
Paisley – A Liverpool Legend
The Liverpool Job
Not Just Another Club: Manchester United

British Library Cataloguing in Publication Data
A catalogue record of this book is available from the British Library
ISBN 0-947808-86-8

published in Great Britain by   Soccer Book Publishing Ltd.
                                  72 St. Peters Avenue
                                  Cleethorpes
                                  N.E. Lincolnshire
                                  DN35 8HU
                                  England

Printed in Great Britain by Redwood Books, Trowbridge, Wiltshire

CONTENTS

INTRODUCTION

EDSON Arantes do Nascimento (otherwise known as Pelé) called it The Beautiful Game; Danny Blanchflower, who led Tottenham Hotspur to the classic, League-FA Cup double at the start of the 1960's, called it a game of imagination and improvisation; and author and broadcaster Hunter Davies called it The Glory Game. The name of the game, of course, is football, and it is a game which has undergone a startling transformation through recent years, as money has begun to count for more and more.

By the end of 1995, a game called Rugby had also undergone an astonishing transformation, as the cash began to flow, and when England tackled South Africa at Twickenham the match attracted a capacity crowd of 78,000 ... in stark contrast to a Soccer friendly between England and Switzerland at Wembley three nights previously. That match had pulled in an audience of some 30,000, and the Daily Mail's noted columnist, Ian Wooldridge, was prompted to observe: 'English Soccer can hardly give away tickets for Wembley, whereas the glittering new Twickenham temple would treble that (78,000) crowd, if accommodation were available'. Wooldridge also wrote: 'The match will generate more than £2 million and, for the first time ever, the players will legitimately receive their modest cut'. Then came the sting in the tail: 'Professionalism, naturally, incurs new responsibilities. Rugby players should study how Soccer players conduct themselves and do precisely the opposite'. Ouch!

On another page, Wooldridge's colleague, Neil Harman – the paper's chief football writer – brought to our attention the current face of English football, which he regarded as 'a sorry sight ... How complacent the game has become, as arms are raised higher, morals slip lower, and excuses become richer'. And as he cited close on a dozen instances of stories which had hit the headlines for all the wrong reasons, during the weeks of November, 1995, he concluded: 'There is no saving grace in any of these cases. Of themselves, they will not precipitate the end of football's world; but, collectively, they eat away at the fabric of a game which has long been in peril of sacrificing what shred of public sympathy it has left'. Few could deny the truth of his words.

Public sympathy? – That is a commodity which has been in short supply over many years, in one respect ... when it come to the business of being on the side of England's various football managers, going back to the mid-1940's, when Walter Winterbottom first took charge of the national side, and coming bang up to date as England prepared for the European championships of 1996 and – one hopes – the World Cup finals of 1998. Terry Venables, whose England career as a coach had been clouded with controversy, was about to make his exit, and the Football Association was striving to come up with the name of the next incumbent, who would be the ninth man to take charge of England affairs on the pitch.

Of the eight managers up to and including Terry Venables, I got to know some fairly well and made the acquaintance of others. I learned about Walter Winterbottom through the eyes of Ronnie Clayton, who captained England as the successor to Billy Wright. I knew Joe Mercer, who confided to me that football – 'my very lifeblood' – had brought him to his knees. Sir Alf Ramsey? – He once gave me an exclusive interview – and looked at me as if I had done something stupid when I asked him a particular question. Bobby Robson? – I have long held him in high regard, not least because he did me a particular favour. And when Graham Taylor was a club manager, I always found him approachable at the post-match inquest.

This book is about the men who have managed England's international side, and therefore it spans half a century. Some recollections are personal, although generally the story is of the fortunes, and the fluctuations in fortunes, of teams and their managers.

Bobby Robson and Terry Venables have both talked about loyalty … Don Revie (whom I knew well) was accused of disloyalty when he defected to the United Arab Emirates. Sir Alf Ramsey inspired total loyalty among his players … and I knew a fair number of those who won the World Cup for England in 1966. Jack Charlton, Gordon Banks, Alan Ball, Roger Hunt, Nobby Stiles and company. They were the first and, so far, the only men to have carried off the glittering prize, and in recent times England's hopes have been dashed more than once. Yet hope springs eternal, and the 1998 World Cup gives England another chance. As for Terry Venables, he was spelling it out what the European championships of 1996 entailed, when England played host. He insisted that he had the players who could make an impact, and he talked about his own responsibility: 'The onus is on me … we have got the players, and it is up to me to get the game-plan to suit us'. Time alone, of course, would tell if El Tel had got it right.

CHAPTER 1

LONG BEFORE Terry Venables became arguably the most controversial of the managers who have occupied the hottest seat in football – the England job – the position was described as 'one of the great Walter Mitty jobs; practically everyone who has any interest in football indulges in daydreams of running the England team. There are more saloon-bar managers than there are armchair generals'. In 1996, as England were striving to emerge victorious from the European championships, I was listening to someone who reckoned the national team boss has 'the hardest job in football'. That description came from someone who was talking not only from experience, but with hindsight … Peter Swales, who had four years as chairman of the England-international committee and who, by then, had served on the committee for no fewer than 23 years.

Swales was one of the men who interviewed Don Revie, Ron Greenwood, Bobby Robson and Graham Taylor for the job of England manager and he told me: 'It was a job which destroyed Don Revie; Bobby Robson didn't like it one little bit; and Graham Taylor had to live with it'. Robson himself has indicated that, had things gone differently, he would have liked to stay on as the national team manager – so why, then, did Swales say Robson 'didn't like it one little bit'? – The answer, in a nutshell, was the aggravation Robson (and he wasn't alone) had to endure from the media; and Swales pulled no punches when it came to talking about the media and its influence upon people. Swales himself came under fierce criticism from the media as England faltered and flopped, while trying to qualify for the finals of the World Cup in the United States in 1994; he also suffered from the barbs directed at him during his chairmanship of Manchester City.

By the spring of 1996, England had had eight full-time team bosses, overall … in order, they were Walter Winterbottom, Alf Ramsey, Joe Mercer, Don Revie, Ron Greenwood, Bobby Robson, Graham Taylor and Terry Venables. Winterbottom's reign lasted from 1946 to 1962, and during that time England played 137 matches. They won 78 of those games and drew 31. Ramsey's time lasted from 1962 to 1974, which meant he was in charge of the national team for 113 games, of which England won 68 and drew 28. It was Ramsey, of course, who achieved lasting fame as the one manager to have steered England not only to the final of the World Cup, but to glory as they triumphed. Remarkably, for a man whose clipped tones seldom betrayed even the slightest of emotions, it was Ramsey, also, who went right out on a limb when, at a Press conference in London, he proclaimed: 'England will win the World Cup in 1966. We have the ability, strength, character and, perhaps above all, players with the right temperament. Such thoughts must be put to the public, and particularly to the players, so that confidence can be built up'.

Rarely, if ever, can there have been such a public act of faith by a manager in his team; but for Ramsey, his players and the fans who followed their fortunes, his proclamation turned out to be prophetic – it came true. Since when successive managers have been expected to follow this class act … and have been villified time and again; even if, as in the case of Bobby Robson, they came so close to emulating the 1966 World Cup winner. In the case of Joe Mercer, there was never any expectation that he would lead England to World Cup glory, because he was called upon to do what amounted to a caretaker job during 1974. Under Uncle Joe, as he was affectionately referred to, England won three and drew three of the seven matches they played. Then, along came Don Revie, whose tenure of office began in 1974 and came to an abrupt (and controversial) end in 1977 when he went off to a highly-paid job with the United Arab Emirates. The manner of his departure left the Football Association not only bewildered, but expressing righteous indignation as Revie left its officials to pick up the pieces. During his time in charge of the England team, there had been 14 victories and seven defeats in the 29 games played. Revie, of course, had his own reasons for leaving the job of national team manager, and he made them public, to some degree, but it is interesting to see what Peter Swales had to say about him.

'To start with, he was one of the best club managers of all time – but, as it turned out, he wasn't suited to the England job. Revie was an awful England manager. Don't ask me why he wasn't suited to the job, but for one thing it simply isn't the same as being a club manager.' At the time that Joe Mercer was about to take his leave after his temporary stewardship, three other managers – Gordon Milne, Gordon Jago and Jimmy Bloomfield – were in the frame as possible successors; but once Don Revie had indicated, quite clearly, that he fancied a crack at the job, the Football Association felt that there was no real need to look any further. If Alf Ramsey had been handed the job after having achieved success with Ipswich Town, Revie's claims were – or appeared to be – absolutely impeccable, after what he had achieved with Leeds United. By the time he was on his way to the Middle East, his reputation had been tarnished considerably, in the eyes of many people back home.

The next incumbent was Ron Greenwood, and he held the job down from 1977 to 1982, when he made way for former Ipswich manager Bobby Robson to chance his arm and try his luck. Robson's term of office lasted from 1982 to 1990 and, according to the man himself, he would have been prepared to carry on after that, given the right kind of encouragement. But when it was made clear to him that there could be no guarantees, he decided that it would be prudent for him to look elsewhere and so, even before England had completed their 1990 World Cup expedition to Italy, Robson knew that he would be returning to club management – this time not with Ipswich or any other English club, but with PSV Eindhoven in Holland. By

1996, Swales – who had seemingly been one of Robson's sternest critics in the past – was telling me: 'I always felt that Bobby Robson wasn't a good England manager – but in the end, he went close to winning the World Cup, and I have to admit that now I look at him in a different light'. A candid admission from someone who himself had to take a great deal of what people in football call 'stick' over his own record as a hirer and firer of managers.

Indeed, there was one occasion when Swales, with a somewhat wry smile, told me as he looked back on those occasions: 'I can't half pick 'em!' And he also admitted that 'the biggest mistake I made was to sack Tony Book'. Yet the then chairman of Manchester City showed loyalty, too, as he kept Book on the backroom staff … and while Swales departed from Maine Road, Book was still there as Venables did his bit for England.

During the era of Ron Greenwood, England played 55 matches, and they won 33 of them while drawing a dozen; and during the era of Bobby Robson, they played 95 games, winning 47 and drawing 29. They also went to the semi-finals of the World Cup in 1990, and lost out only in a penalty shoot-out against West Germany. By that time, of course, the team manager of England was the man who had the responsibility for picking the players who would line up for the start of a game – which was not the case when Walter Winterbottom was appointed back in 1946. Winterbottom, a bespectacled, scholarly gentleman in appearance, was also, in some aspects, a man before his time. He hailed from a Lancashire mill town – Oldham – and was first appointed as the Football Association's director of coaching, subsequently becoming the first manager of England's international side.

It may cause eyebrows to be raised now, but in the early days the England management had actually been shared round by members of the Football Association Council, on an alternating basis with, it should be added, the assistance of a club trainer. When Winterbottom was appointed as the manager, as well as the director of coaching, it meant that he would in effect be doing two jobs for the price of one. At a later date, Bobby Robson would have something to say about getting money out of the Football Association. When it came to Winterbottom – the first national team boss to put his head above the parapet and be in the firing line – Ron Greenwood had something to say about this man. Greenwood himself was a deep thinker about the game and, as a club manager at West Ham, he had demonstrated that he could produce a team which played enterprising, entertaining and fluent football – even if, as some critics averred, the team lacked a streak of steel in its make-up. Greenwood it was who declared that Winterbottom's influence upon English football was still being felt, long after he had gone through the exit door. According to Greenwood, the Winterbottom influence 'touched many of the clubs from which England called on players to win the World Cup in 1966'. And others felt the same – even if, as happened with Graham Taylor, the United States inflicted a defeat upon England which called for a black border round the story in one newspaper. Ironically, Alf Ramsey was a member of the England side which, during the Winterbottom era, suffered that shock defeat at the hands of the so-called no-hopers of the United States.

If Peter Swales changed his mind to some extent about Bobby Robson, he remained firm about Graham Taylor – who, by the summer of 1996, was back at Watford – as he said: 'Graham didn't have the players, he didn't get the breaks and yes, he did make a few mistakes. But I still feel that he would have made it, had fortune been kinder to him'. Taylor, of course, went through the England exit door, although the Belo Horizonte defeat of England by the United States in 1950 didn't lead to the sacking of Walter Winterbottom … he was given a vote of confidence to carry on, and he lasted for another dozen years. In fact, the year before Winterbottom did go, one of today's television pundits, Jimmy Hill – a former player and, by 1996, the chairman of Fulham – was offering the view that not only was Winterbottom a talented and honourable man, but that he deserved to succeed in any profession. There was a sting in the tail. 'Unfortunately, he has chosen possibly the most difficult job in England. More criticism has been hurled at this one invidual than at any other five men in the football game put together'.

Even so, the game hadn't at that time got to such a stage where the manager of the England team would be derided as 'Turnip head' and be slated mercilessly while he was still striving to achieve some sort of success in the job. Peter Swales had quite a bit to say to me about what he considered to be the worst thing about being the manager of England, and it applied not only to Graham Taylor, but to his predecessor, Bobby Robson. If Robson appeared to be at odds with Swales by saying he would have liked to stay in the job, while Swales reckoned Robson 'didn't like it one little bit', this explanation from the former chairman of the England-international committee says a great deal. 'Bobby Robson's greatest aggravation came from the media, or from some sections of it, at any rate – in fact, probably the worst thing about the England job is the media. It doesn't matter whether you're winning matches or losing them … you will find that someone is getting on your back.

'If every other paper was for the manager of the England team, one of them would still be against him – even if he were winning. There's always someone who has to be different. Without a doubt, the greatest pressure of all comes from the media. Some of the media take it upon themselves to have a go at the manager, come what may. Robson had to take a lot of stick, and Graham Taylor suffered terrible abuse. We don't support our England managers – and by that I mean the media'.

'I don't think the fans are so bad, but they are influenced by what the papers say – and that's the reason why half the people who might well be qualified for the England job shy away from it. If you're a club manager, sure … there is pressure on you, especially if you're in danger of being relegated. But even that is nothing like the pressure on the man in the England job – and that's something you just cannot get

around. You would have to win the World Cup and the European Championship …
and even then, someone would be against you'. Swales could speak from first-hand
knowledge of pressure from the newspapers, because during his lengthy spell as
chairman of Manchester City, and as chairman of the international committee, he was
often under fire. Never more so than during the final months of his chairmanship at
Maine Road.

There, the fans were calling for him to quit in favour of a former playing favourite,
Francis Lee, who was quoted thus: 'If they gave trophies for cock-ups, you wouldn't
be able to get inside our boardroom'. According to Lee, it had been Swales who,
years earlier, had sold him (against him wishes) to Derby County. Lee's parting shot:
'You'll regret this …' Eighteen years on, after having savoured a championship success
with Derby, Lee was about to depose Swales from the job he had held down, often
amid acrimony, for two decades. 'The chairman's been there so long he thinks he's an
institution', said Lee. And when he did succeed to the Maine Road throne, his accession
was greeted with cheers from 30,000 fans … a plane towed a banner which read,
'Welcome, Francis Lee', and thousands of blue-and-white balloons rose into the sky
as the one-time City striker stepped into the directors' box. But after three months of
season 1995-96, the picture was looking much more grey and Lee was admitting: 'I
have never run an unsuccessful company before, but this has been different to anything
I have known'. It was a season in which City were fighting for Premiership survival.
Yet when I talked to Peter Swales and asked him how he felt about City's problems,
he declared: 'I'm still a City fan at heart, and I still want them to do well'. If Swales
had hired and fired managers, he had remained consistent and unswerving in his
support for the club, even after bowing out. And even though he had suffered in
various ways before that day arrived.

For instance, one of his former managers (and he had seen half a dozen depart
during his chairmanship) came back to cast a shadow. Howard Kendall, who himself
was to suffer as a team boss – and who had once been in the frame for the England
job – had returned from Bilbao to take charge at Manchester City and, at that time,
Swales told me: 'I've got the best'. City were struggling, but Kendall began to turn
things round – then he rocked his chairman by telling him that he wished to rejoin
his first love in football, Everton. Swales told me: 'Once that happened, I realised
that no matter how much I wanted to keep Howard – and I did – there wasn't a great
deal of point in standing in his way. It's not a good thing to hold someone when you
know he won't be happy'. So Kendall went back to Everton – and returned with his
new charges to Maine Road. Everton inflicted a 5-2 defeat upon City, and that day
was a black one indeed for true-blue Peter Swales.

The irate home fans vented their displeasure on him, and – this was the last Saturday
of season 1992-93 – some of them pelted the City chairman with eggs. As the chants
of 'Swales out! Swales out!' rose on the air, City's chairman found his new, blue jacket

was being stained by egg yolk, and he required protection from the club stewards. He said: 'I don't mind the booing – I can take that – and I expect criticism. But I don't like people throwing things. Even so, it was a bad result, and I feel deeply for the fans. I understand their feelings'. I once interviewed Gordon Taylor, the chief executive of the Professional Footballers' Association, and as he talked about the state of football he came up with a pretty damning indictment of club chairmen in general – while not pulling any punches when it came to laying some blame at the door of Peter Swales. Since it was such meaty stuff, I tackled Swales about it and, somewhat to my surprise (and to his credit), he went along with quite a bit of what Taylor had said although, as I had expected, he did defend himself, as well.

Swales also defended himself against one of Don Revie's former stars, Johnny Giles, who had become one of his fiercest critics during the early 1990's. Giles gave the then City chairman a hard time of it in print – so much so, that Swales was stung into rapping back as he said: 'In all my years in the game, I have never felt so incensed about a piece of reporting'. To which Giles (whom I have known even longer than I knew Swales) replied: 'I stand by every line of my criticism.'

Giles had accused Swales of appointing managers, then denying them the power to manage; Swales retorted that he had always supported his managers 100 per cent – 'in fact, I have probably given them too much freedom, when you analyse the spending I have authorised'. Swales also declared: 'If allowing managers to get on with the job was a fault, then I am guilty'. As the pressure on Swales to quit increased, the situation turned somewhat ugly ... the police advised him to maintain a low profile and to employ a minder. After Swales had gone from Maine Road and Lee had been installed as the supremo at Manchester City, Lee admitted that as the club struggled during season 1995-96, at times it had felt 'like trying to climb Everest with people tugging at the rucksack'. Maybe more than one of the men who managed England experienced similar feelings, on occasion.

The late Sir Matt Busby was a man who experienced management at two levels – club and country – and when he was asked once by the great Billy Liddell about management, he replied: 'I have made my bed, and it turned out to be a good one ... but not many managers can say the same as me'. Phil Neal, capped 50 times by England and a player who won just about everything with Liverpool, experienced the ups and downs of management with Bolton Wanderers, Coventry City and Cardiff City, and he was at Graham Taylor's shoulder during Taylor's final months in the England hot seat. Neal told me: 'Sooner or later, we all face the sack. A lot of managers think they're strong enough to leave the worries of the job behind when they go home, but they cannot really do that'. Kenny Dalglish quit his job at Liverpool the day after having seen his team draw 4-4 against Everton in an FA Cup-tie at Goodison Park, and he left Liverpool sitting on top of the table. But when he sprang the shock news to chairman Noel White (now chairman of the England-international committee) and chief executive Peter Robinson, it was with the admission that he could no longer carry on ... the pressures of the job had got to him.

In tandem with Malcolm Allison, Joe Mercer enjoyed the days of wine and roses at Manchester City (where Peter Swales was then the chairman) but, like Dalglish, he had experienced the other side of the coin, with Sheffield United and Aston Villa. Joe used to recount the story of his problems at Villa Park, as the club suffered relegation and, as he was sitting in his office, with his head in his hands, a telegram was brought in to him.

It came from Dick Wragg, who at the time was chairman of Sheffield United (he was also Swales's predecessor as chairman of the international committee), and – as had happened to Villa, during Mercer's time there, so it had happened previously to Sheffield United ... they had been relegated. As he opened the telegram, Joe felt for a moment that here might be a message of commiseration; instead, the telegram read: 'Congratulations – you've done it again'. Like Kenny Dalglish, Joe Mercer suffered from the anxieties of football management – indeed, he once told me that the stresses of football – he called it 'my very lifeblood' – had driven him to a state of nervous exhaustion. By the time he had returned to football, as Manchester City's manager in 1965, he had learned a great lesson. He had been out of the game for a year, 'and maybe, in retrospect, that illness wasn't such a bad thing. I learned patience'. Joe's motto by then had become: Make haste slowly.

During the mid-1990's, by which time he was managing in Portugal, Bobby Robson was reflecting upon a health scare which had appeared life-threatening. Suddenly, he was told he needed an operation, and the news shook him to the core. After it was all over, and he had survived to carry on managing, he recounted what Bill Shankly used to say about football being more important than life and death. Robson said that he had come to realise Shankly's statement had not been true, after all – even though Robson himself had considered for years that football was virtually the be-all and end-all of his own existence.

Peter Swales was not a member of the committee which interviewed Terry Venables for the England job because, as he told me, 'I was right in the middle of the takeover business at Manchester City, and that put me under a great deal of pressure. So I opted out, when it came to the England side of things at that time, and Noel White stood in for me'. By the time the European championships were looming, Venables had made it clear that he would not be looking to carry on as England's team boss, and – naturally – after a great deal of speculation about his future, the media talk was of his possible successor. Names were strewn around like confetti ... Kenny Dalglish, Howard Wilkinson, Dario Gradi, Frank Clark, Glenn Hoddle, Gerry Francis ... the only snag seemed to be that one after another, people were shying away from the opportunity.

One of Venables' lieutenants, Bryan Robson – by then the manager of

Middlesbrough and himself being put forward as a candidate by some folk – urged the Football Association to do its utmost to get Venables to reconsider his decision to go; he also urged Venables to think again. And the problem of finding the right man to succeed Venables and spearhead England's World Cup venture was not the only one on the agenda ... the Football Association appeared to be having trouble in finding someone to become its technical director, and there was debate as to who would follow Sir Bert Millichip as chairman of the assocation if and when he stepped down after the European championships.

It was Gordon McKeag, president of the Football League and himself a member of the FA Council, who summed up the job of chairman as 'a balancing act ... in these times of change and challenge, whoever becomes the new chairman of the FA has, above all, to be a man of integrity, a man of courage. There will be unpleasant decisions to be made from time to time and, where appropriate, he has got to be prepared to stand up to the more powerful football barons. He has got to be a man of diplomacy, to effect compromise, to balance the views of everybody and then seek to get all of them to agree to the best way forward'. It made you stop to think, that such a Soccer sage must come from among the list of those on the FA Council ... apart from Sir Bert Millichip, there were no fewer than 89 members. One senior member of the FA Council confessed: 'I've been wracking my brains for six months, and I can't think of anyone who can do it'.

It seemed to be a problem not dissimilar to that which faced the association in its efforts to come up with the name of someone who could stay the course as technical director for 10 years or more. Going back to the question of a new chairman, Gordon McKeag said it was 'vital' that whoever was elected should understand 'the delicate balance between the professional game – and the tensions within it – and the pyramid of football outside the professional game'. Millichip himself suggested at one point that 'while no-one is more aware of my age than I am (he was 81), my resignation is not a *fait accompli*'. He was further praised for 'his many acts of diplomacy during a 15-year term notable for its self-effacing willingness to put the good of the game before self-promoting gimmicks'.

The writer went on: 'What matters most is having the right man for the job (of chairman), be he 41 or 81, not any old chairman of the politically-correct age. Millichip is not hanging on for the sake of it, like some stubborn, old carbuncle. A man of dignity and scruples, he neither needs, nor deserves, all the uncouth, gratuitous insults' (the writer here could have been referring to the incumbent of the national team manager's job). 'Honest Bert' was quoted thus: 'I will continue beyond this summer's election only if a substantial majority of the council think it would be in the best interests of the game'. A yardstick which had already been touched upon by Gordon McKeag, who made another telling point ... 'One of the major differences coming in today, rather than 15 years ago when Bert became chairman, is that you are having to deal with a new breed of powerful chairmen who are not football people'.

Bert Millichip may have been in his early 80's ... Brian Clough, at the age of 60, was reported to be ready to throw his hat into the ring for the England manager's job (a post for which he had been interviewed some years earlier). But it seemed that Clough, like several others, was not a serious contender by the time the 1996 European championships were on the horizon. As for the position of technical director, the Football Association's chief executive, Graham Kelly, was observing: 'If we can't find an Englishman who is able to do the job, it seems a bit of a slight on English professionals. The technical director will be in charge of all playing matters in England – we are about raising standards and fusing the two strands of the FA's activities ... the international team and the coaching department. We need to have a situation where there is effortless transition between those who are coached properly at ages eight to 10 and the full England team. We need someone of stature who also has a presence and a track record so he will be accepted by the professional game'.

Kelly again: 'He also needs an appreciation of educational work, though we want a football person before a teacher. It is no good having the best coach in the world if he can't organise all the things that need to be organised within the FA. The professionals and technicians agree – English players are not as good as the best Europeans. Our players don't practise at an early age – say, eight onward – as they should. They play too much competitive, 11-a-side football.

'It was traditional until 18 months ago that they could only have an hour with the best coaches at the schools of excellence. It took us three years of hard negotiation to change that. All the time, we were fighting against the obstacles of vested interests'. In fact, after various names had ruled themselves out of the running for this particular job, it was reported that the Football Association might well need to draw up a new short list. It was said that Leeds United manager Howard Wilkinson had become the fourth man to say 'Thanks, but no thanks' when he was interviewed for a job which, seemingly, would be worth some £3,000 a week. 'I couldn't let the situation go on, and I felt it only fair to speak to the FA about my feelings', he said.

Wilkinson was considered by many to be the ideal candidate ... a former school teacher, he had played as a professional, become an FA staff coach, coached and managed various England squads. At club level, he had managed title winners in the Northern Premier League and in the Football League, and in the spring of 1996 he steered Leeds to the final of the Coca-Cola Cup. On the eve of that final against Aston Villa, Wilkinson was saying: 'Criticism? – That guts you. But the older I get, the more I say it – a lot of clubs in this country are self-destructing. It's got to be recognised that for every top, there's a bottom, for every winner, a loser'. And when it came to the job of managing England? – 'At Sheffield Wednesday, my response was, "Everybody would like to be England manager" ... and I was told I shouldn't be discussing ambitions when I had a job to do. Last time at Leeds I said "No", and my ambition was questioned. This time, I've made a conscious decision to say nothing – and still I'm being psychoanalysed'.

By that time, Wilkinson had come to the conclusion that the 'older man' in football was 'less likely to be affected by what people think of him … he won't be attracted by certain aspects of the job and won't have an overwhelming need to play five-a-sides'. He recalled working with the then England manager, Bobby Robson … 'walking round the pitch after a bloody boring friendly against Wales at Wembley which England had won. He turned to me and said, "That'll keep the natives quiet for a few weeks."' Wilkinson was a man who, at close quarters, had seen the pitfalls of managing the national team, and he was not afraid to express his opinions.

For instance, on the people who wield power: 'I think some of the people who work on FA councils make fairer and more analytical decisions than people who have a vested interest. I'm not sure that letting the most powerful people have the power is for the good of the game. There is a very definite difference between power, influence and wisdom. I'm only too aware of the jealousies and suspicions that exist in football … you don't need to be a rich club to be greedy. A desire to protect your own interests at all costs is predominant in football. You have to bring in legislation that governs behaviour. People will cut corners in an attempt to be winners. They have to be shown that will not be tolerated. There haven't been too many visionaries in football during my lifetime – they're the type of people we need now. And for the good of the game, let's make sure there are some good young players to entertain us … without players, you have no games.'

On the eve of season 1995-96, Wilkinson was reflecting that management 'has always been a precarious profession – but nothing like it is today. The pressure … has intensified out of all proportion. To be manager of a club for more than two years is a considerable achievement'. In May, 1992, when England won the race to stage the 1996 European championships, Sir Bert Millichip had declared: 'I hope this can be the start of a brighter era for English football'. Early in season 1996-97 he was out of a job… Since then, England had failed to make it to the finals of the 1994 World Cup, after failure two years earlier in the European finals.

There were some intriguing views expressed by various people in the game. Gordon Taylor, for instance, on the way forward in the international arena, as he declared: 'England's national team are attempting to rebuild their reputation, but this will be even harder if this influx of (foreign) players continues'. Former Arsenal goalkeeper Bob Wilson revealed that at Arsenal, costly Dutch star Dennis Bergkamp was the last one in from training sessions 'by a good hour or so', while Lee Chapman, whose experience as a striker had included Stoke City, Arsenal, Leeds United and a spell in French football, claimed that English teams had been 'found wanting in technical ability'. There was more: 'English players generally regard it as a punishment when they are brought back in an afternoon', whereas Continental players viewed things differently.

According to Chapman, an extremely articulate fellow, the English player's European counterparts 'generally go back twice a day – and they expect to do that. They concentrate on their technical skills'. And whatever you might think of Monsieur Eric Cantona at Manchester United, according to his manager, Alex Ferguson, he was 'first in, last out' at training ... not only that, but his influence in this respect was rubbing off on to his team-mates. It was reported, too, that the Continentals were more aware of the need for careful attention to diet and drink than players in this country – 'physically, they've caught up and, in many cases, overtaken us', said former Leeds and Manchester United striker Joe Jordan, who also played for AC Milan.

According to Gordon Taylor, England's failure to qualify for the 1994 World Cup finals indicated that the Premier League wasn't working out as people had hoped. 'I want us to be a major player on the world stage ... The Premier League was formed with a view to making sure that the England team is at the forefront of our game'. Then he declared: 'Two years on, and we haven't qualified for the (1994) World Cup. I may be wrong – I hope I am – but the inevitable consequence of the Premier League is a contraction of clubs, jobs and supporters. It's a change, but I don't know whether it's progress'. His verdict: 'I would do away with the Premier League – I much preferred the old system, which was fair. Three quarters of the money going on a quarter of the clubs? – The equation isn't quite right, for me'. Taylor's arguments were featured in a 10-point analysis in a magazine.

The chief executive of the Professional Footballers' Association said it had invested heavily in preparing a report into coaching, both in England and abroad. Former Everton and Manchester City player Paul Power – not only a qualified coach, but a lawyer – had been investigating why countries such as Holland ('with less resources and smaller population', said Taylor) were able to produce good players and succeed at international level. 'I just hope the FA are able to take on board its recommendations', said Taylor.

One man who summed up pithily the qualities required for making a success of the England job was former Manchester United and England winger Steve Coppell. He himself became a manager with Crystal Palace and, as an ex-university graduate, has plenty of sense. According to Coppell, the England job 'needs the patience of Job, the creativity of Da Vinci, the diplomacy of Kissinger and the foresight of Nostradamus'. There seems to be no answer to that ... and, of course, many folk wondered how Coppell himself would fare, when in October, 1996, he took charge of struggling Manchester City.

CHAPTER 2

ENGLAND team-boss Walter Winterbottom took his skipper to one side and told him, 'You are still the tour captain'. A message which Ronnie Clayton, already the holder of 35 caps, appreciated, because it indicated he wasn't out of the international reckoning for good. He was wrong. After a shambles of a match against Yugoslavia, which England had drawn 3-3, the headlines had fairly screamed: 'Clayton must go!' And go he did, although, as Winterbottom had told him in Madrid, he remained captain while the tour of Spain and Hungary followed the debacle at Wembley. Ronnie told me later: 'The funny thing is that I never tried harder than I did against Yugoslavia … but sometimes when you try your hardest, things only get worse'. The year was 1960.

Winterbottom knew what it was like to be taken to task by the media, and he broke the news gently to the player who had followed Billy Wright (England's captain a record 105 times). Winterbottom reminded Clayton that he had had a long, hard season with Blackburn Rovers (who had just lost the FA Cup to Wolves at Wembley), and that a rest would probably do him good. His timing of tackles was a split-second slow, he was failing by inches to reach the ball. And so Johnny Haynes became the new skipper. Clayton told me: 'When the team was announced, Walter walked over and shook Johnny by the hand. Several of the sportswriters applauded. Fair enough. But there was one item to which I took exception – when Johnny was made skipper, I was supposed to have acknowledged his honour with a curt nod. In fact, two minutes later I walked over, shook him by the hand and wished him and the boys the best of luck. Johnny thanked me for that.' And according to Clayton, 'the only thing wrong with that tour was that England lost against both Spain and Hungary'.

Clayton also took exception to some criticism about his display against Yugoslavia. As he told me: 'It just shows you can't see and hear everything from a seat in the stand'. He had been accused of giving two team-mates an ear-bashing … 'in fact, I was NOT shouting at them … I was urging them to stop shouting at each other! They had begun to have words, and I told them to stop it and get on with the game'. As Ronnie admitted later, that match was his downfall – 'after it, I knew I was a likely candidate for the chopper'. And the chopper fell, for good and all. He had progressed from Under-23 level to the senior side, seen Billy Wright switch to centre-half as he took over Wright's right-half spot, then emerged as captain in his own right. His first cap had come in 1955, against Northern Ireland (a 3-0 win), and as he stayed in the side England beat Spain 4-1, Brazil 4-2, Finland 5-1, Germany 3-1, Wales 3-1, Yugoslavia 3-0, Denmark 5-2 (a World Cup qualifier), Scotland 2-1, Eire 5-1 (another World Cup qualifier), Denmark 4-1 (the World Cup return), Wales 4-0, France 4-0,

Scotland 4-0, Portugal 2-1, Russia 5-0, Scotland 1-0 and the United States 8-1.

Of course, there were a few reverses; but in 30 of the 35 internationals in which Clayton played, he finished on the losing side only half a dozen times. As for Walter Winterbottom, that 8-1 thrashing of the United States must have been balm to his soul, because back in 1950 his England side had been unceremoniously dumped off the World Cup trail in Belo Horizonte, as the unrated United States scored the one and only goal. Billy Wright had skippered England that day, Alf Ramsey was at right-back, and Tom Finney was there, as well. Wright, captain in 90 of his 105 England outings, still had vivid memories of the debacle, even when he was nearing 70. 'What made it harder to take was that the Americans were amateurs, and their football wasn't organized. The public read about it in the newspapers, and the newspapers were edged in black. It was a bad performance – no argument about that. But it was a game we should have won ... we had the chances. We lost, history was made – and they will never let us forget it'. Wright was in the England side which later beat the United States 8-1, but 'no-one remembers that now. They only remember the defeat at Belo Horizonte'. England's team that disastrous day: Williams, Ramsey, Aston, Wright, Hughes, Dickinson, Finney, Mannion, Bentley, Mortensen, Mullen.

Back in 1950, three World Cup matches ended with England coming home with

Walter Winterbottom who was the first England team manager.

their tails between their legs, because as well as having done the unthinkable (losing to the United States), they had been beaten by Spain, although they had managed to defeat Chile, 2-0. England's record in their qualifying group had appeared impressive enough – maximum points from their tussles with Scotland, Wales and Northern Ireland (14 goals scored, only three conceded), but Belo Horizonte in Brazil in June was, as a contemporary report put it, 'England's most humiliating moment', and a dejected goalkeeper, Bert Williams, was pictured standing on his line and looking with horror as the effort from centre-forward Larry Gaetjens went past him. If Sweden were rated giant-killers by virtue of their 3-2 victory over Italy – the Swedes were coached by Englishman George Raynor – it was recorded that 'the real shock was England losing to the hotch-potch USA'. The goal was described thus: 'This humiliating defeat was sealed after 37 minutes; left-half Walter Bahr crossed into the goalmouth, Williams failed to gather cleanly, and the oncoming Gaetjens deflected the ball in with his head. England had been unimpressive in beating Chile, but it was a scintillating performance compared with this shattering shambles'.

Like Wright and Finney, Alf Ramsey played in all three matches in Brazil and, of course, he had no notion then that in 1966 he would mastermind England's successful bid for World Cup glory. In Winterbottom's day, Belo Horizonte was not the only black mark on England's copy-book, because in 1953 the Hungarians visited Wembley and walked off the famous turf not only victorious, but being hailed as the Magical Magyars, after having inflicted a 6-3 defeat upon the home country. Once again, England's side included Wright and Ramsey, along with Stanley Matthews and Stan Mortensen (who had played in all three of the 1950 World Cup games). Against Hungary, Matthews and Morty had Blackpool team-mates Ernie Taylor and Harry Johnston in support. I knew them all – Johnston became a newspaper colleague of mine, Matthews once told me: 'I hope you don't sleep tonight…' This was when my paper was running a story Stan would rather have seen put on the spike. My conscience was clear, and I answered him: 'Stan, I can assure you … I'll sleep like a babe in arms'.

Stan had done nothing wrong, and neither had I – the story concerned his proposed testimonial match at Stoke – but it led to his giving me the cold-shoulder for a couple of years or so. Then, after he had become Port Vale's manager and was about to lose his job, he asked if my paper would be interested in doing a series of articles. Going back to Hungary, the Magical Magyars hit England with seven goals in 1954 … Wright and Finney both played, but Ramsey had been replaced by Ron Staniforth, while Manchester United's Roger Byrne was in at left-back. Tommy Taylor and Duncan Edwards had yet to arrive on the England scene (Edwards and Ronnie Clayton became close friends and roomed together).

The Munich air disaster robbed England of Edwards, Byrne and Taylor, while Wright finally hung up his boots and another England man, Jeff Hall, had his career cut short by polio. Walter Winterbottom had to reshuffle the pack and get on with trying to achieve success in the World Cup – although, of course, Wright was there for the 1958 expedition to Sweden, as was Don Howe, who followed Hall at right-back. Bobby Robson was at inside-right, and Ronnie Clayton played just one game – the last one, which England lost 1-0 against Russia. Earlier, England had drawn 2-2 against the Soviet Union, 0-0 against Brazil (the eventual champions) and 2-2 against Austria. But Northern Ireland and Wales gained the glory, when it came to assessing British performances in Sweden … although Walter Winterbottom still remained the boss. In fact, he lasted four more years.

Ronnie Clayton had a high opinion of him, and of the way in which he treated his players. As for Winterbottom's record, by the time Clayton was on his way out England's record against foreign teams at Wembley, from the end of the war to 1960, read like this: Played 28, Won 19, Drawn six, Lost three. And that included the Hungary debacle in 1953. One of the men who played up front for Winterbottom was Bolton's Nat Lofthouse, and in a match against Finland he scored twice, to overhaul the immortal Steve Bloomer's 28-goal record, which had stood for 45 years. Lofthouse also earned the soubriquet 'Lion of Vienna' for his courageous display in a game against Austria.

At one stage during Winterbottom's up-and-down reign, Wales had caused some consternation by beating England 2-1; but the team had bounced back to lick Northern Ireland, Spain, Brazil, Finland and Germany (on their own territory), and had drawn against Scotland and Sweden. The team's performances had prompted the great Sepp Herberger to say, after the victory over Germany: 'England are a world football force again'. The team which did England proud that day: Reg. Matthews, Jeff. Hall, Roger Byrne, Ronnie Clayton, Billy Wright, Duncan Edwards, Jeff. Astall, Johnny Haynes, Tommy Taylor, Dennis Wilshaw, Colin Grainger. However, what goes round comes round, and England had to endure defeats, as well as victories. As Clayton told me later: 'Since that win in Germany, our World Cup hopes have gone up in a puff of smoke yet again; what's more, we've taken a series of humiliating defeats in South America and been the whipping-boys for the critics who travelled with us on that disastrous tour'. But, as Ronnie also said: 'If we've had our failures abroad, our home record shows other countries have also had them … against us'.

Clayton defended his manager as he pointed out that Winterbottom had lost key players such as Edwards, Byrne, Taylor, Hall and Wright – 'one of the wisest footballers I've ever known' – and asked: 'How can any country take a mauling like that and expect to carry on staging victory after victory, at home or abroad? – Key players cannot be replaced overnight; the replacements must be given time to strike a blend'. Clayton also told me: 'When I became captain of England, I made a vow that I would try to keep a level head – and the same size in hats – and tackle my problems as Billy Wright tackled, and overcame, his'. Wright played all his 105 internationals under Winterbottom, so they forged a lasting partnership, and this was what the

England team boss had to say about his long-time skipper: 'He forced himself on my notice in the most subtle way. When reflecting on a match and assessing who had played well and who had played badly, almost invariably I decided that Wright had played well. It was the regularity with which he forced himself into the team... In those early days, one never thought that here was a future captain of England. Yet one could be assured that around him could be built themes of play, and his captaincy grew from the fact that here was a man whose consistent game could be integrated with other players and link him solidly to them – players like Scott, Swift, Franklin, Lawton, Carter, Matthews and Mannion'.

Ronnie Clayton gave me examples of the Wright way of doing things. 'When a player was capped for the first time, Billy always took the trouble to get to know him … I remember being capped for the first time, and before the game, against Northern Ireland, I was in the Under-23 side against Yugoslavia at Maine Road. Billy travalled from Wolverhampton not only to see the game, but to get to know his new England colleague'. Twice Wright lost his usual, genial expression, as Clayton recalled. The first concerned his romance with Joy, of the famous Beverley sisters. There was tremendous media interest, and Ronnie said: 'There were stupid jokes about Joy meets her Mr. Wright. Billy knew the romance alas bound to attract a lot of publicity, but I gained the impression that sometimes he found the banter – some of it not in the best of humour – was being taken too far'. Another time, during a match, 'keeper Reg Matthews, who had been given some harassment by the opposition, began to handle crosses and shots rather uncertainly. 'Reg. dived for a ball and Billy, so far as the watching thousands were concerned, rushed to cover him. The fans didn't see, but the players close to Reg did … Billy gave him a pat on the back and urged him to "snap out of it". That encouragement worked, because Reg began to play like his old self '.

There's an old saying that a prophet has no honour in his own country, and this could often be said about the men who have managed England – starting with Walter Winterbottom, whose reign began with a remarkable, 7-2 victory over Northern Ireland in 1946. There were wins over Eire and Wales, then came an 8-2 thrashing of Holland. It was 1-1 against Scotland in 1947, 3-0 against France, then the first defeat … 1-0 by Switzerland. There followed an astonishing backlash … a 10-0 triumph over hapless Portugal; then it was 5-2 against Belgium, 3-0 against Wales, 2-2 against Northern Ireland and 4-2 against Sweden, to see out 1947. In 1948 England beat Scotland, Italy (4-0), Northern Ireland (6-2), Wales, Switzerland (6-0) and drew with Denmark, while the following year, it was 1-3 each time against Scotland and Sweden, then 4-1 against Norway and 3-1 against France. Surprisingly, Eire won 2-0, but England bounced back to beat Wales 4-1, Northern Ireland 9-2 and Italy 2-0. There was no inferiority complex – and no shortage of goals – around that time, as the World Cup loomed in 1950. Scotland, Portugal (5-3) and Belgium (a 4-1 defeat) paved the way for the World Cup matches.

From the beginning of season 1950-51 to the end of 1951, no fewer than a dozen players came to the end of the international line as they retired, one by one, and in the four years to the 1954 World Cup, when Wright claimed the centre-half spot as his own, there were nine candidates for the job. Gil Merrick followed Bert Williams in goal, Alf Ramsey lasted until six months before the World Cup, and while Finney and Matthews vied for the right-wing berth, left-wingers on show included Mullen, Medley, Robb and Elliott. Despite losing his place on the eve of the World Cup, Lofthouse regained it during the series. He had been the hero of a dramatic, 3-2 victory in Vienna two years earlier, and after a four-match absence between 1953 and 1954 he returned to figure in the line-up for the World Cup opener against Belgium.

That game was one of goals galore – eight of them altogether, with the rivals claiming an equal share. If the defence could be faulted for having leaked four goals, the attack could be credited with restoring the balance; and a 2-0 success against the host nation, Switzerland, gave cause for optimism. That was dispelled, however, as Uruguay pumped four goals past Merrick, who took some of the blame for England's defensive errors. The forwards managed to score twice, but England, having reached the quarter-final stages, were once more on their way home. And in eight games overall (against FIFA, Hungary twice, Scotland, Yugoslavia, Switzerland, Belgium and Uruguay) 28 goals had been conceded, with 20 scored. It was generally considered that England had done less well than in Brazil, bearing in mind that the European climate suited them better. For Winterbottom, two things stood out – that he needed more time with his players before internationals, and the team itself would need to be built up again, with players coming through from the Under-23 side.

At that stage, those conducting the post-mortem looked ahead and broadly agreed with the proposed new strategy, while at the same time looking for greater co-operation from clubs. The names of Edwards, Sillett, Flowers, Revie and Quixall came into the reckoning, as did those of Clayton, Blunstone and Perry – indeed, on the same day that England played Northern Ireland, Clayton and Haynes both graduated front the Under-23 side to senior status. England were to go through 16 games without defeat, and Clayton, Haynes and Edwards played in every match, barring injury. A team-mate of Clayton's, Bryan Douglas, also emerged from an Under-23 tour in 1957 to claim a senior spot.

Two players from West Brom also made their mark – Don Howe and Derek Kevan, a powerful inside-forward who became the most controversial figure of the 1958 World Cup finals in Sweden. In 1955 England scored seven goals against the Scots, five against Denmark, four against Spain; and in 1956 they hit Brazil with four goals, while Finland went down 5-1 and – for the second time in a couple of years – Germany lost to England. By the time the World Cup qualifying matches had come round again, England were kicking off with a 5-2 success against the Danes, following three-goal victories over Wales and Yugoslavia, and there were four more wins and a draw before a defeat by Northern Ireland. Overall, Denmark conceded nine goals in their two World Cup qualifiers against England and Eire conceded half a dozen.

Hard on the heels of a 4-0 win over Wales came a reminder that anything can happen in football – Northern Ireland's 3-2 victory made people stop to think. But as England cruised to a 4-0 win against France and a similar success against the Scots, followed by victory over Portugal, optimism once again became the order of the day. However, the fans were made to blink a bit when Yugoslavia beat England 5-0 and Russia drew 1-1 on the very eve of the 1958 World Cup finals. There was more than a touch of irony in the fact that the organizing committee of the world championships was assembling from every part of the globe in Stockholm, where the winter snow lay thickly on the ground. The committee had gathered to make the draw for the World Cup, and the date was Thursday, February 6, 1958 … the very day that Manchester United's team, with its galaxy of international footballers, was being decimated on a snowswept runway at Munich.

Among the dead were Edwards, Byrne, Taylor and another England player, David Pegg; and casualties included potential World Cup footballers such as Bobby Charlton Dennis Viollet and Albert Scanlon. Eddie Colman, another possible for Sweden, had been among these who did not live to tell the tale. Edwards, Byrne and Taylor had each played a score or more international matches, so they would most certainly be missed, and while Bobby Charlton came into the reckoning, as he played in three World Cup warm-up matches, his time was still to come. The 5-0 defeat by Yugoslavia in Belgrade was accompanied by temperatures in the 90's … Bill Slater said that after only 15 minutes he felt drained, with his head swimming and his legs feeling as if they were made of rubber. Clayton, it was said, had perhaps the worst match of his life'.

For Walter Winterbottom, it became a case of make-do and mend after the air disaster at Munich; yet there was hope, because after a draw against Russia in Moscow, the first World Cup match would be against them, too. England had learned, 48 hours after Munich, whom they must meet in Sweden … Russia, Brazil and Austria. And when the finals got under way, they kicked off with the least-experienced team of all 16 nations competing. Goalkeeper McDonald, left-back Banks and right-half Clamp had each played for his country just once; Robson had played twice; on the other hand, Wright and Finney were going into their third World Cup finals … and Brabrook and Broadbent were about to undergo their international baptism of fire.

Fortune did not favour Winterbottom and his players, as they drew 2-2 with Russia, 0-0 with Brazil and 2-2 with Austria to go into a play-off against the Soviet Union. It turned out to be third-time unlucky against the Russians, as the Soviets enjoyed the one necessary bounce of the ball. That made all the difference between England going through to the quarter-finals and going home. Twice, with the Russian goalkeeper a beaten man, England scoring efforts rapped against a post ... and each time, the ball bounced clear. Once, the Russians managed to hit a post ... and this time the ball rebounded into the net.

Once more, then, Winterbottom had to look ahead and live in hopes that by the next World Cup, in 1962, he and his players would have got it right. After Sweden in 1956 England met Northern Ireland and drew 3-3, trounced Russia 5-0, drew with Wales 1-1 – and then began to suffer somewhat, because during 1959 they lost three successive matches after having beaten Scotland and drawn against Italy. Brazil won 2-0, Peru slammed four goals past England, and Mexico beat Winterbottom's team 2-1. It was left to the United States, vanquished 8-1, to give England's players some feeling of satisfaction.

After the 1958 experience, the question was asked: 'Can England win the world championship – ever?' And the answer came: 'Despite a domestic system which does not help the building and development of strong international teams, it can be done. If the 1958 team had reached the semi-finals – which was certainly not beyond the bounds of possibility – we would all have been pleased, not to say boastful. But to savage the team because it went out by a solitary goal after a match as close as the one we had with Russia, and dismiss the team as a failure, is simply absurd'.

One of the great controversies surrounding England's performances in Sweden concerned the omission of Bobby Charlton and Brian Clough, and the choice of Derek Kevan. When it was all over, the inquests still raged on, amid an atmopshere of considerable acrimony – even bitterness. It was recorded that 'emotion, prejudice, false judgment – many other factors impinged on the arguments made for and against these players'. Kevan, regarded as the typical England centre-forward – the battering-ram type, some would claim – had never been on the receiving end of a good press since his international baptism against Scotland, in 1957. His critics claimed he lacked even the elementary skills of the game; that he was clumsy, sometimes fell over the ball, and yet he was powerful enough to force defenders to come to him ... he was 'a player who could browbeat a defence, break it down and score goals'.

Charlton? – Apart from the obvious question about the completeness of his recovery from the horror of Munich, there was the question of whether or not he could turn in consistent, all-round performances, as well as score dazzling goals. Against the Scots, in April, 1958, he had hit a magnificent debut goal, but otherwise failed to sparkle; and a similar criticism was levelled over his display against Portugal in the May. What was called into question was the work-rate factor, the need to graft for 90 minutes – and it was claimed that 'in such a situation, England could not afford specialist players'. As for Clough, he had scored 40 goals for his club, Middlesbrough – but that was in the Second Division. Furthermore, if he were to go into the England side, the entire attack would need to be remodelled to accommodate his style of play. Or so the argument ran. Otherwise, Clough himself would have to adapt – and that would need time … which England by then had not got.

In the event, Bobby Smith became Kevan's deputy, as Kevan won the vote for Sweden; Charlton, too, travelled, but made way for Robson, and Clough was the odd man out altogether. Charlton was considered for outside-left in the play-off game against Russia, but Alan A'Court kept his place. And so the 1958 World Cup came and went, with England returning home amid fresh controversy. Oddly enough, just a year earlier, the critics had been saying that Kevan should be in and Clough should be out.

Another point was made – that 'the England team with apparently the least talent was the team which achieved the best performance – in 1954 it reached the quarter-final round. The England team with apparently the most talent was the team which achieved the poorest performance – in 1950, when it was a case of much skill and talent, but not enough determination'. A charge later to be levelled by Sir Bobby Charlton, in some respects, as he talked about the poor display of Graham Taylor's World Cup falterers against Norway. Back in 1958, the cure-all was seen in this manner: 'Victory for England can only come as the result of a process of rebuilding. We must select young players and feed them on a diet of international experience at every level, and make them international players. Persistence with youth is the only way forward. It can be done, England's turn will come'. As it did in 1966.

Before that day dawned, however, Walter Winterbottom had one more shot at bringing home the World Cup bacon, even though there was one thing going against his team from the start … they would have to meet and master the finest footballing sides in the world not in Europe, but much further afield – in Chile. And, as before, it turned out to be a task which was too much – indeed, 1962 proved to be the end of Winterbottom's reign as the international team boss. Not that it looked that way as England produced results on the way to South America. They were in the qualifying group with Portugal and Luxembourg, and they emerged as the top team, with seven points, after a 9-0 romp in Luxembourg (and 4-1 in the return), a 1-1 draw in Portugal and a 2-0 victory on home soil.

In the finals in Chile, England were pitched in with Argentina, Bulgaria and Hungary (who led the party with five points, while England headed Argentina into second spot, on goal difference). England's sole success was a 3-1 win over Argentina, who beat Bulgaria and drew with Hungary. The Hungarians hit Bulgaria for six, which gave the critics of England some ammunition, since Winterbottom's team could do no more than draw, 0-0, with Bulgaria, while they went down 3-1 against the Hungarians. In the quarter-finals, Brazil beat England 3-1, the Czechs beat Hungary 1-0, and in the final itself it was Brazil 3, Czechoslovakia 1. One more World Cup had been and gone, one more effort by England had ended in disappointment for the players and their manager.

So Winterbottom finally made his exit from the international arena, and he did so with people having mixed feelings about him, in many respects. There was no doubt about his commitment, his integrity and his knowledge of football; neither is there any doubt that he had to work under great difficulties, especially during his early days. His 'purple patch', it was said, came during season 1960-61 when his 4-2-4 plan shattered Northern Ireland, Luxembourg, Spain, Wales and, finally, Scotland (who were hammered 9-3). And, as Ron Greenwood said, he left his mark in a manner which benefited future England teams and managers. It is interesting to see how the one-time chief executive of the Football League saw Walter Winterbottom – and two of his successors, as well.

Alan Hardaker, whom I got to know well, could be irascible and, at times, a bit dogmatic – he was a Yorkshireman, blunt in speech, candid in opinion and a fellow who could call a spade a bloody shovel. Hardaker saw Winterbottom as 'tall and scholarly, a dedicated theorist but lacking the kind of background and steel the job demands'. Winterbottom, in fact, had started out in football as a half-back at Manchester United, but back trouble curbed his ambitions of making the grade. Originally, he had trained to be a teacher, and this aspect tended to show through when he was talking football. Hardaker's assessment was that he did a better job than might have been expected, considering that he had not experienced management or international football before being appointed as England coach. He suffered one great disadvantage from the start – while he acted as adviser when it came to picking the England team, the international committee had the final say. Strong on theory and certainly dedicated to his job, Winterbottom – according to Hardaker – was 'never quite a part of the earthy world of the professional footballer'. I know exactly what Alan meant – some of his phrases were entirely new to players whose vocabulary, in many instances, was rather more limited. And players can be the greatest mickey-takers in the business … as was instanced in a famous story about the England coach whose reign spanned four World Cup Campaigns. The tale ran that while talking to his players he brought into the conversation a move which began with the right-back, involved three more players and ended with the right-winger crossing the ball to the far post, where the centre-forward would then nod it home. At that point, the centre-forward asked: 'Which way would you like the lace pointing?'

If the story is true, then Winterbottom would have appreciated that spark of humour from someone who, probably, was not as erudite or articulate as himself. Alan Hardaker reckoned that he was not the person to get the best out of the players under his command at that period of tine – not least because coaching was still considered to be something not only new, but 'clever', so far as established stars were concerned. They knew how to play the game … and, of course, the game has evolved and come a long way since those post-war days. Some would say the game has not improved, in many respects. Ronnie Clayton, probably, for one. By the mid-1990's, this one-club man was president of Blackburn Rovers' Supporters Club, and saying:

'We might have had a few more trophies in the cabinet, but I don't think we'd have been as happy anywhere else'. Clayton was saying something else, too; 'I think we'll have better memories than the current crop of players - and you can't buy those. I loved every minute of my career, playing with and against men like Finney and Matthews. We trained morning and afternoon, then begged the trainer to let us carry on a bit longer, because we were enjoying it so much. Now they play too many matches. I don't think today's players actually like playing football any more. It seems to be just another job for them'.

CHAPTER 3

ALF RAMSEY was not everybody's cup of tea – but then, who is? – Among his critics were Bobby Robson and Alan Hardaker, and I must confess that when I did an interview with him once, I was made to feel as if I had just asked a very stupid question. Yet Ramsey's players would hear not one wrong word said about him ... and he, in turn, defended them to the hilt. The Hardaker view was that Ramsey was 'very difficult to understand and work with, a peculiar chap in some ways – but, above all, the man who won the World Cup'. The Robson view was coloured by 'the succession of attacks' he had to endure from the man who, like himself, had enjoyed success at Ipswich. Half a dozen of the men who managed England remain alive, at the time of writing ... Walter Winterbottom, Sir Alf Ramsey, Ron Greenwood, Graham Taylor, Terry Venables and, of course, Robson himself ... who reckons that only these can possibly understand what being manager of England really means, in terms of the problems involved.

Robson claimed – rightly, too – that as a group the men who have managed England should give each other their support; and he said that 'Sir Alf apart, we gave it and got it. Neither Walter, Ron, the late Don Revie nor the much-lamented Joe Mercer ever tried to take me apart' – but he felt that Sir Alf Ramsey 'betrayed that unwritten, unspoken rule by taking myself and my players to task, undermining confidence within the camp and often at crucial times before we set off for a European or World Cup finals'. Strong stuff from one ex-England manager about another. Robson wondered if Ramsey differed from the others because he had been the only one to win the World Cup; 'did he put himself above us, because of it?' Alan Hardaker rated Ramsey thus: 'I have never met another quite like him in the whole of my career' – but in 1966 'the moment was right, the team was right and the man was right'.

No-one could possibly give you an argument about those sentiments, because Ramsey's record spoke for itself. It was recorded that 'it is Alf Ramsey's firm intention to turn England into a team of world-beaters' – and he did. 'He knows his football from A to Z and is seen at his best when the odds seem against him, as when he took little Ipswich from Third Division obscurity to the Division One championship and European football'. It was further recorded that 'when he left Ipswich to become England team manager, his first hurdle was a match against world-champions Brazil at Wembley. England gained an encouraging draw. Ramsey's men then proceeded to gain heartening victories in Czechoslovakia, East Germany and Switzerland, and returned home to defeat the Rest of the World in the special match to commemorate the Football Association's 100th birthday'.

My own, personal memory of Sir Alf Ramsey is of the day, around 1970, when I travelled by train from Liverpool to London especially to do an interview with him – and I was appreciative of the fact that he was willing to give me the time. I wasn't feeling in such a happy frame of mind by the time I arrived at Euston, because before I boarded the train at Lime Street I had slipped off the edge of the kerb and twisted my ankle badly – so badly that it swelled like a balloon and was causing me great pain. I tried to make light of it as we talked, but it wasn't easy as I did my best to concentrate upon what the great man was saying, in answer to my questions. He was just as I had seen and heard him on television … the accent was clipped (he had once taken elocution lessons), the stare was direct, and the manner was somewhat stern.

When we discussed the 1966 World Cup triumph, I put a question about the team and the tactics; in my view, it was a sensible question to ask, and I was somewhat taken aback when, giving his answer, the implication appeared to be that I had asked a damn-fool question. Apart from that, however, the interview went down well enough and I was able to give Sir Alf a good spread in the sports edition of my paper the following Saturday. One thing I did learn from our chat – that, as with Bill Shankly, it was a wise man who thought before he spoke, when trying to get answers from Sir Alf Ramsey … and even then, as Alan Hardaker said, you could make a mistake.

Hardaker recalled a 2-1 victory over England by Scotland, and – 'attempting to say something tactful' – he mentioned that if England had to lose, it was better that they lost against the Scots than against foreign opposition. The reaction from Ramsey? – 'I thought he was going to explode with rage'. Finally when he could bring himself to speak, he said: 'I'd sooner anybody beat us than the bloody Scots'. Hardaker also recalled that there were times when Ramsey, as manager of England, 'did not get a fair crack of the whip' – this, when it came to the support he received (or, rather, didn't receive) from some club managers as the League did its best to rearrange fixtures and so make things easier for England.

No doubt about one thing; as Hardaker said, Ramsey was a professional in charge of professionals, and he was 'the boss'. First and foremost, he won the right to choose which team England fielded, and his record was impressive indeed. Just as his record at club level had been before he landed the England job. He had played at full-back for Southampton and Tottenham Hotspur and, while no greyhound, he had shown that he could read the game and make the best use of his positional sense. Along the way, he played 32 times for England, and when he became manager at Ipswich he steered them from Division 3 to the League championship in just six seasons – something which, by any standard, was outstanding.

By 1966 he had formulated the way to win the World Cup – a 4-3-3 formation which became christened as 'the wingless wonders'. Not that everyone approved of this plan; indeed, during the World Cup itself one prominent administrator felt impelled to observe that should England win the trophy, 'it may be the worst thing

Sir Alfred Ramsey – England's most successful manager to date who led his team to success in the 1966 World Cup

that could happen to English football'. Well, they did – and clubs copied the system which, it must be admitted, put the accent on efficiency, rather than entertainment. But results are all, especially in the World Cup. It has been argued that while Ramsey's team at international level could make the system work very well, the clubs who became copy-cats in many cases couldn't make it work, because their players hadn't got the same ability. And there is some force in that argument. Not that Ramsey himself ever told clubs that they should emulate the tactics and team formations he had applied with such singular success at international level.

They say that success breeds success, and that is true; at the same time, as Joe Fagan told me after his spell as manager of Liverpool (in his first season he accomplished a unique treble), once you have succeeded, you are expected to carry on from there. And once England had won the World Cup, Ramsey and his players were expected to retain it. By October, 1973, England were up against it, as they met Poland, and while Brian Clough had termed the Polish 'keeper 'a clown', it was this man who somehow kept out every England effort, with the result that our World Cup dreams vanished overnight. England's failure to qualify for the finals in Germany brought about the end of an era, because in the spring of 1974, Sir Alf Ramsey was given the sack. One view offered about his fall from the pinnacle was that he had been loyal too long to the players who had brought him such acclaim, and that he had merely tinkered with the system he had been using, right the way through. It was said that 'he would not accept change' and that the writing had been on the wall for a long time.

Ramsey also suffered as Walter Winterbottom had done, from the attentions of the media, once things began to go less than right. And, of course, by the time 1974 had come around, the Football Association was concerned about the financial aspect of World Cup failure. There had been criticism of the fact that while England had claimed the World Cup in 1966, the money made from this tournament which had been staged in England was much less than had been hoped for. The profit motive, as well as the glory, had come to matter more and more with the passing years and the increased demands within the game.

Alf Ramsey was born in 1920 at Dagenham, in Essex, and he won selection for Dagenham Schools against West Ham Schools. After leaving school he played for a team which went by the name of Five Elms (he was then a centre-half) and while there he was spotted by a scout from Portsmouth. But though he signed amateur forms for Pompey, he never did play for them, and it was while playing football in the Army that he attracted the attention of Southampton, who invited him to join them … after having stuck 10 goals past the Army side! His first outing was against Luton Town, and though he gave away a penalty, the Saints still won. Ramsey was not to know it then, but he was on his way to fame.

It was Southampton manager Bill Dodgin who recognised that in Ramsey, he had a player who could switch with good effect to right-back, and as time went on, that was the position in which Ramsey made his mark. Ramsey had made Manchester City's international ace, Sam Barkas, his role model, and not only did he produce some accomplished displays which led to his emergence as a potential international himself, he showed that he was a student of the game. As he progressed, so did the Saints, because in Ramsey's first season he savoured the excitement of helping them in their bid to achieve promotion. Season 1947-48, his first full campaign, didn't end in triumph, however … Southampton had to settle for finishing in third place, so Newcastle United and Birmingham City went up. There was consolation for the full-back from Dagenham, though – he learned that he was being taken on a tour of Europe as a member of the England B squad.

No more than four months later, Ramsey's highest hopes were being fulfilled, because he was selected to play for the full international side, and as England flexed their muscles, and employed their skills, against the Swiss, he was able to enjoy playing in a team which scored half a dozen goals without reply. Two years on, and Ramsey was leading Southampton, as they sought once again to reach the higher echelons of English League football – but then he was injured, and so he lost his place. Ironically, the injury came during a friendly match against Portsmouth, the club which had first shown interest in him, but that meant little to Ramsey as he was informed by Southampton's manager, who had had to reorganise the side after the injury, that regaining a first-team place might well prove to be very difficult. Ramsey was sufficiently upset by this news that he decided to cut his ties with the Saints, and after asking for a transfer he was on his way – though not to Sheffield Wednesday, who were quick to seek his services.

He chose Tottenham Hotspur, then in the Second Division, and the deal – involving cash and another player – went through with the total money estimated at £21,000. Ramsey's old club, Southampton, were to miss the promotion boat again at the end of that season … by a solitary point. Meanwhile, his arrival at Spurs happened to coincide with the development by manager Arthur Rowe of a style of play which became known far and wide as 'push and run' football. Like Ramsey, Rowe – once a Tottenham player – was a student of the game.

In Rowe's side were three players who would make their names as managers … Ramsey himself, Bill Nicholson and Vic Buckingham. Like Rowe, Nicholson was to achieve lasting fame as a team boss at White Hart Lane. Meantime, all three became an integral part of the Rowe footballing machine which involved passing the ball around at speed, and with great accuracy. It was a game made for Ramsey, with his ability not only to read situations even before they arose, but to spray accurate passes to team-mates. And as they played, so Spurs stormed through the Second Division, with Ramsey making it third-time lucky as the club finished with 61 points, which put them nine clear of their closest rivals. And back at The Dell once more, it was doom and gloom, as Southampton were pipped for promotion on goal average. Tottenham Hotspur went through their First Division fixtures as they had gone through their games in the Second … opposing teams scarcely knew what was hitting them as they sought to fathom out ways and means of stopping this slick, quick-passing side. Season 1950-51 turned out to be another successful campaign, because Spurs lost only seven League games as they surged to the top and took the championship. In three seasons as he enjoyed conspicuous success, Ramsey missed no more than five matches, and as he became a regular on the international scene he also took over the captaincy at Spurs. It was at a time when England were about to test their strength in the World Cup, and FIFA decided that the home-international championships should be used as a qualifying eliminator, with the top two nations going through to the finals. And that was how England went into the World Cup, while second-placed Scotland, having decided perversely beforehand, refused to reverse their decision not to go, because they had finished second. Salt was rubbed into the wound as England, already assured of qualifying, beat Scotland by the only goal at Hampden and thus robbed their great rivals of a share in the home championship. Exit Scotland from the World Cup.

So Alf Ramsey came under the influence of Walter Winterbottom … and found himself in the firing line, along with his team-mates, as England lost that World Cup match against the United States in Belo Horizonte in 1950. The American team was considered to be on a loser from the start – so much so that the players felt they could afford to go partying on the eve of the match.

They certainly didn't appear to be suffering from a hangover as they struck shortly before half-time, and somehow their defence managed to cling on and repel everything England could throw at them – and that was plenty. The 1-0 result brought humiliation and shame to the players and manager Winterbottom, although in time they showed that they could carry on living – and playing. Ramsey himself helped to restore a little of the gloss to England's record by emerging as a player who could step up and slot the ball home from the penalty spot in tense situations – he hit a late equaliser against Austria, scored from the spot again against the Rest of the World in November, 1953, and he was also in the England side hammered 6-3 at Wembley by the Magical Magyars of Hungary. The return game ended 7-1 in favour of the Hungarians, and so the myth of English supremacy in the game we had given to the world was finally destroyed.

As the mid-1950's approached, so there was a decline in fortune at club and international level. Arthur Rowe was in failing health, Spurs became an ageing side, and opposing teams finally learned how to deal with push-and-run football. When Rowe was replaced by another former Tottenham player, Jimmy Anderson, it was the signal also for Ramsey to find himself surplus to requirements, as newcomer Danny Blanchflower was given his chance. Blanchflower was to lead Spurs to the classic, League-Cup double at the start of the 1960's. In the meantime, Ramsey saw the writing on the wall, so far as his playing days were concerned, and he decided to see if he could embark upon a career in management.

This was the point at which Ipswich Town came on the scene. They had been relegated, after having achieved a brief moment of fame when, in 1938, they had gained promotion to the Third Division (South). They hung on in there for 15 years, finally made it to the Second Division – then, after just one season, they slipped back down again. And this was where Alf Ramsey came into their calculations. His brief was to turn Ipswich Town into a football club which was recognized as being rather more than a nonentity tucked away in deepest East Anglia. To the surprise of many people, he achieved the desired result in quick time – Ipswich totalled 59 points and so they claimed a place in the Second Division again. They spent the next three seasons more or less in mid-table anonymity, although Ramsey was busy working out the next stage in their progress.

He certainly didn't have the spending power to go out and sign top names, but he did have the brains to work out a tactical formation – later to become known as 4-4-2 – which made the best possible use of the players at his command, and in addition he instilled into his players a fierce sense of belonging to the club and of loyalty to each other – and to their manager. As a result, this closeness helped in no small measure when Ipswich took on their supposedly superior rivals, and they showed that their system worked, when it came to scoring goals. They had two wingers, Jimmy Leadbetter and Ray Stephenson, who could beat their men, and in Ray Crawford and Ted Phillips they had a couple of strikers who knew how to make use of the service they received – the proof of the pudding was there for all to see, as Ipswich Town rounded off season 1960-61 with a record of 100 League goals scored, and the championship of the Second Division.

Even then, Ipswich were regarded with some amusement by people who thought themselves to be better; so far as their critics were concerned, Ipswich Town Football Club was up from the country and, in all probability, would soon be put in its place. But Ramsey's 'country lads', who were in the £25-a-week bracket, demonstrated they were not there for the taking, after all. While Spurs, under Bill Nicholson, had done the double with a side which cost quarter of a million, Ramsey's homespun Ipswich was valued at around £30,000, in terms of transfer fees overall … and the signs looked ominous when Manchester City hammered them 4-2 in their First Division baptism of fire. Gradually, however, Ipswich showed that they could survive, and with Crawford and Phillips still scoring goals they crept up the First Division table. Walter Winterbottom, in fact, became so impressed by the efforts of Crawford that he decided he was worth a place in the England team, and he was called up to play against Austria and Eire. Which meant that unfashionable Ipswich could now boast that they had a second international in their ranks – Ramsey, as a former England player, having been the first. As for the League, Ipswich fans knew that the late-October game against Spurs was crucial, because it would show if their local heroes were up to going for the championship – or if they would be put in their place. Tottenham travelled to Ipswich – and there they were conquered. The final scoreline: 3-2. And in the return, Ipswich triumphed again, this time, 3-1.

The two victories by Ipswich could arguably be said to have robbed Spurs of the double; instead, they had to settle for the FA Cup. In the event, Tottenham wound up their season with a total of 52 points (14 fewer than during the previous campaign, when they had won 10 more matches) … while Ipswich rounded off their historic season by totalling 56 points. It may have turned out to be the lowest title-winning total of the decade, but for Ramsey and his players there was no argument about it – Ipswich were the champions. And as it happened, Ramsey's rise to footballing fame as a manager was about to coincide with the fading out of Walter Winterbottom as

England's team boss – coupled with the fact that, after their title-winning campaign, Ipswich Town began to fall from grace.

Not to put too fine a point upon it, Ipswich had been rumbled – rival teams now had fathomed out how to match and master them, and they were on the slippery slope back to the Second Division. First, they slid down the table until they were third from the bottom; then, in season 1963-64, disaster overtook them as they dropped to the bottom rung of all and, as they conceded no fewer than 121 goals, they were relegated. But by that time they were under new management, because Alf Ramsey had switched his allegiance from club to country ... although his was not the first name in the frame for the England job. Winterbottom, as he bowed out, suggested that Burnley manager Jimmy Adamson would be the man for the job. But Adamson decided in his wisdom that managing England was not for him. Meanwhile, the Football Association decided not to turn to established team bosses such as Stan Cullis (Wolves) and Bill Nicholson (Spurs); instead, they went for the man who had turned unfashionable Ipswich into a First Division force.

By October, 1962, the Football Association had acted; an approach was made to Ipswich chairman John Cobbold, seeking permission to talk to Ramsey about the England vacancy. Reluctant as they might be to part company with the man who had done so much for the club in such a short space of time, they felt that there was no way they could bar Ramsey's route to further glory – the England job then was still considered to be the pinnacle for ambitious team bosses. And so he walked out of Portman Road for the last time, as a local hero, and embarked upon the stage which was to make him a national hero.

CHAPTER 4

ALF RAMSEY'S make-up may have been a composite of many things, and there may have been times when, with his clipped accent and his unblinking stare, he tended to rub people up the wrong way. But he appeared to have an unshakeable belief in his own destiny, and as he rode the criticisms during his early days as manager of England, he gathered around him players who would not hear one wrong word spoken about him. I came to know more than a few of them well ... Alan Ball, Gordon Banks, Jack Charlton, Nobby Stiles, for instance; and always, when we talked about England, Ramsey and the World Cup, they sang his praises. And it could not be said that all Ramsey's players were Yes-men.

Ramsey started out as England were embarking upon their quest for success in the European Nations Cup. They were taking on France, and for the first time since 1958 (when Yugoslavia had scored a nap hand of goals) England conceded five goals, while managing to score two. Ramsey's half-time pep-talk hadn't been sufficient to turn the tide – but he was to put that right in no uncertain terms, come the final of the World Cup in 1966. Meantime, he concentrated on getting to grips with his new job and, in this respect, he kicked off with one advantage over his predecessor; he was the boss ... he picked the team. He also had one advantage over his rivals from abroad ... while he might become the target for some hard words, from time to time, he would never have to endure the kind of thing some of his managerial rivals had to suffer. In Brazil and Italy, for example, the fans tend to be much more volatile than the more phlegmatic British – or, at least, they did 30 years or so ago.

Many people considered that in 1966, Brazil were kicked out of the World Cup; be that as it may, after they had been knocked out, back in Rio de Janeiro an effigy of the Brazilian team coach, Vicente Feola, went up publicly in flames. As for the Italians, who were tamed by unrated North Korea, their team was pelted with tomatoes on returning to the land of the lire. At Ipswich, Ramsey's major signing had cost something like £12,000; as England's manager, he had the pick of the finest players in the land – club demands permitting. His old boss at Spurs, Arthur Rowe, told Ramsey that 'it's easier to run the England side when you're picking from the top players in the country ... at Ipswich, you're always fighting people with gates twice your size'. Rowe's view: England could not have made a better choice.

After the game against France, England took on Scotland – and lost, 2-1, Ramsey maintained that 'we missed far too many chances ... if just two or three of them had been accepted, we could have won'. One month later, England tackled Brazil and managed a draw, although the critics were quick to point out that Brazil were without Pelé, Garrincha and Zito. After that, Ramsey's team went on a roll ... a 4-2 victory over Czechoslovakia (who had been unbeaten at home for five years); a 2-1 win over East Germany (always rated as stern opposition); and an 8-1 avalanche of goals against the Swiss, with Bobby Charlton hitting a hat-trick. So Ramsey and his players returned from their tour on top of the world. As to his insistence that England not only could, but would win the World Cup (he had first said this to a journalist at Ipswich, then at a Press conference in London), Arthur Rowe explained the apparent dogmatic expression of belief this way ... It was 'an expression of fierce desire and a subsequent conviction ... it was no cheap, throw-away phrase; it was studied'. Possibly, maybe probably, Ramsey was intending to instil such belief into his players right at the outset, by making it clear that he himself was unwavering in his conviction that the job could be done. And when the moment came for him to lift the troops, at the end of normal time in the World Cup final against West Germany, he responded with the right words and the players rose to the occasion. As the saying goes, cometh the hour, cometh the man.

During that summer tour of 1963, when the Czechs, the East Germans and the Swiss all wilted against England, Ramsey experimented by playing Charlton and Terry Paine as wingers; later, he was to switch Charlton to more of a midfield role as England became known as 'the wingless wonders'. Victories over Wales, a FIFA eleven and Northern Ireland (this one an 8-3 outing) had the fans thinking that Alf Ramsey was the miracle man, and one noted sportswriter was prompted to observe that 'Ramsey is surprising his critics'. Not least when it came to the art of communication with the media ... although, later, that viewpoint would undergo a change. Meanwhile, England's team boss was starting to gather around him the players who would win the World Cup ... Gordon Banks, Bobby Moore, Bobby Charlton, Ray Wilson. At that time, also, it appeared as if Jimmy Greaves would figure boldly in the 1966 tournament – but he was to suffer a massive disappointment as, in the final analysis, Ramsey plumped for Roger Hunt.

When England scored that 8-3 victory over Northern Ireland, it was their sixth success on the trot, and the scoring ratio was 26 goals for, only three against. Greaves was a four-goal hero, Paine a hat-trick man. Early in May, 1964, England defeated Uruguay 2-1, and this success cane only a matter of weeks before what was termed 'the little World Cup' was scheduled in Brazil. At that stage, Greaves was in the side, while Johnny Byrne and George Eastham were firm candidates for the World Cup itself. Before the 'little World Cup', however, there was a match against Portugal – a friendly, to celebrate the Portuguese Football Association's 50th birthday. It was the occasion for someone north of the border to say some harsh words about the England manager and the tactics he was employing. Ramsey himself had demonstrated that he was never happy if the Scots should succeed against England ... now Bob Kelly, the outspoken chairman of Glasgow Celtic and the recently-retired president of the Scottish Football Association, had his say. Like this: 'They (the England players) are puppets.

Ramsey pulls the strings, the players dance for him. I think he has theorised them out of the game. They mustn't think for themselves, mustn't deviate from the plan. They have been so brainwashed by tactics and talks that their individual talent has been thrust into the background'. And so Ramsey took his England players to Lisbon for the friendly against Portugal ... and it was there that they gave their answer.

The fact that Portugal were England's oldest allies did not prevent Ramsey's team from doing the talking for him – as it happened, half a dozen of the side facing England that day would be lining up against them for a semi-final in the World Cup two years hence. Five of the England players also took part in both games. In Lisbon, Liverpool winger Peter Thompson was given his first cap, while Byrne emerged as a hat-trick hero as Ramsey's side won by the odd goal in seven. Names such as Torres, Simoes and Eusebio were to become as well-known in England as those of Banks, Charlton (Jack and Bobby), Ball, Stiles and George Cohen, who was in the side which beat the Portuguese. One week after that impressive display, England made rather harder work of beating the Republic of Ireland 3-1 in Dublin – but when England went abroad for the 'little World Cup' they raised eyebrows as they rammed home 10 goals against the United States, for starters. That was ample revenge for the 1-0 blight of Belo Horizonte in Winterbottom's World Cup days, and hopes were high that Ramsey's men could go on to do the business against Brazil three days after the footballing massacre of the Yanks.

There had been one incident which demonstrated, quite clearly, that while Ramsey would always be loyal to his players, he expected absolute loyalty in return. On the eve of the departure for the game in Portugal, several players had gone out to a London restaurant – which meant they were breaking curfew. They returned to find that in each case, the player's passport lay on his bed – a silent message of displeasure from their boss. Nothing was said – until the team had arrived in Estoril ... then Ramsey laid down the law as he told the offenders: 'If I had enough members here to make up a team, none of you would play – you'd all be on the plane on the way home. I realise I can't do this, in the circumstances ... make sure it doesn't happen again'. They did ... indeed, when Bobby Moore (one of the offenders) was accused of having stolen a bracelet in South America, Ramsey was his surest defender. Indeed, as Moore was under house arrest for a time, in Bogota, Ramsey had this to say to the media: 'I shall not smile again until I see him (Moore) walking towards me'. And when Moore did emerge from this crisis with his reputation intact, he went on to demonstrate that he and England's manager had forged a powerful partnership as skipper and team boss.

However, the euphoria of the victories in Lisbon and against the United States was to be pricked like a balloon which had had a pin stuck in it, as Brazil turned on the style in Rio. It was carnival time for the natives, when England suffered a 5-1 mauling by the world champions. Some excuses were made – the heat, the fact that before the game Ramsey's players were stuck inside their dressing-room for around an hour, as the Brazilians kept them waiting (they claimed their coach had been delayed). Whatever, the fact remained that after that victory by the home country, Argentina scored three goals against Brazil without conceding one. So where did that put England in the world rankings? It was during the game between Brazil and Argentina that two events occurred which were to have echoes during the 1966 World Cup … there was something of a rough-house in which Pelé and his direct opponent, Mesiano, figured prominently; and there was the appearance of a player by the name of Antonio Rattin. In 1966, Brazil claimed they suffered unduly from the attentions of opponents – and Rattin was the centre of a furore which involved Alf Ramsey, as he talked about Argentina's behaviour in terms of comparison with animals.

After that hammering by Brazil, Ramsey axed half his team, and England achieved a 1-1 draw against Portugal. Tempers flared as Coluna had a goal ruled out for offside and Torres received marching orders for dissent. England themselves had a couple of goals ruled out for offside but, unlike their opponents, they didn't chase the referee. Portugal were regarded as having scored a lucky goal from a deflection; England's equaliser came from Hunt, who was now coming into the World Cup equation. When England met Argentina in the match which decided which country would win the tournament, they failed to score, so Argentina topped the lot with their 1-0 win which saw them emerge as victors every time out. Surprisingly, only two members of that side – Rattin and Onega – would figure in Argentina's World Cup quarter-final team which met England at Wembley in 1966 … the match which caused such a storm of controversy. Argentina had shown the world that they could adapt, because in their three matches they had employed three different team formations – 4-2-4 against Portugal, 5-3-2 against Brazil, and 4-3-3 against England. Argentina were described as being 'functional' … they were also said to have 'shown their teeth'.

Ramsey's reaction, at the completion of the tournament: 'There is still a tremendous gap between us and them'. Significantly, he added: 'But not a gap that can't be bridged'. He was proved to be correct in that declaration. And he showed during season 1964-65 that he was settling on the side which would do duty for him and for England in the World Cup, most especially when it came to the defence. Banks had nailed down the No.1 spot; Cohen and Wilson were the full-backs; then came Stiles, Charlton (Jack) and Moore which left the five remaining positions to be filled, and it seemed that one way and another, room would be found for Bobby Charlton and, probably, for Greaves. Even so, Ramsey experimented to some tune, as he tried 16 players, including Terry Venables, Alan Hinton, Fred Pickering, Frank Wignall, Barry Bridges, John Connelly, Derek Temple, Mick Jones and, of course, Bobby Charlton, Paine, Greaves, Thompson, Byrne, Eastham, Hunt and a player who would emerge as a hero in 1966, Alan Ball. By then, Martin Peters and Geoff Hurst had still not appeared on the scene.

As for Bally, this pugnacious redhead who epitomized determination, I have known him now for 30 years, and I can remember him telling me how, when he first expressed his wish to play professional football, he vowed to his Dad: 'I promise you I'll play for England before I'm 20'. It was a promise he made good, too … having forced his way into the side at the expense of Eastham, he was celebrating his 20th birthday as England defeated West Germany 1-0 in Nuremburg. Ball, had arrived, and he was to have a long run in the international side, as he won 72 caps. And as Ball became an England regular, Ramsey's team took shape and won matches – during season 1964-65, England suffered not one defeat; there were half a dozen victories, four draws. Like Walter Winterbottom's England teams, Ramsey's players could claim that if they had been totting up points, they would have been in the championship-winning bracket.

But pride goeth before a fall, and there was less than unanimous praise for the manner in which England achieved their successes. For example, they were 4-0 up against Northern Ireland in Belfast … and then they hung on to win 4-3. The one redeeming feature in the eyes of many critics was the hat-trick performance of Greaves. And in the October, when only 45,000 fans went to Wembley, a draw against Belgium was less than convincing.

When England tackled Wales, both teams were shorn of players because of injuries, and the 2-1 win for Ramsey's men was rated as being short of the required standard when it came to the World Cup. Bobby Charlton had been switched from the wing to midfield, and was then dropped, although he would bounce back to achieve lasting fame. When England travelled to Amsterdam for a match which celebrated the Dutch Football Association's 75th birthday, Greaves was the marksman whose goal ensured a draw, and around that time it was recorded that 'it is futile to discuss our prospects in the World Cup … they do not exist'. Some gloss was restored to England's reputation with a 2-2 draw against the Scots at Wembley in April, 1965, especially since Byrne and Wilson were injured, and the season was rounded off with another goal from Greaves – this one won the Wembley duel with the Hungarians.

While his team had been striving to mix results with fluent football, Ramsey had seen his relationship with the media see-saw in a downward fashion, and it was when England embarked upon a summer tour, which kicked off in Yugoslavia soon after the victory over Hungary, that the relationship was summed up by a distinguished sportswriter who, at one time in the future, was to work for the same Sunday newspaper which employed me. Brian Glanville wrote: 'Ramsey clearly wishes the Press would disappear'. Certainly there were some misunderstandings along the way, one of them concerning the fitness or otherwise of Greaves, who was an absentee from the side to play Sweden. When the tour began in Belgrade, Charlton and Thompson were missing (through illness), and Ball replaced Eastham. Paine excelled in that match, which ended 1-1. Then came the 1-0 victory over West Germany in Nuremburg and Paine was in sparkling form again – he was the match-winner, in fact. Four days on, and England were beating the Swedes 2-1 in Gothenburg (their first win in 26 years on Swedish soil), with goals from Connelly and Ball.

The defence, with Stiles emerging as a key player, was settled, but there remained a question mark against the attack, notably at centre-forward, despite the known ability of Greaves as a marksman. Five months after the victory in Sweden, the next match – against Wales – gave Peacock a chance, but there were no goals, and two weeks later England went down by the odd goal in five (Greaves missed three chances, while also hitting an upright). Austria's manager admitted: 'Yesterday I thought England would win the World Cup … today, it is another picture'.

Ramsey had one staunch defender in Leeds United manager Don Revie: 'Alf says he is going to stick to most of his players, and I am delighted at his courage. I still think England will win the World Cup. The important time is next spring, not now'. Indeed it was, and while no-one was overjoyed about the dour display against the Irish in their next outing, at least England contrived to win the match 2-1. The marksmen were Baker and Peacock … both soon to disappear from the international arena. The following month England came up against what was regarded as considerably stiffer opposition, Spain; and suddenly, they were featuring the 4-3-3 formation which was to take them through the World Cup, and producing an impressive performance.

Baker was on the mark again, as England scored twice, and when he retired hurt he was replaced for the second half by international newcomer Norman Hunter. The team which lined up for the start was almost – but not quite – the one which won the World Cup. It read Banks, Cohen, Wilson, Stiles, Jack Charlton, Moore, Ball, Hunt, Baker, Eastham, Bobby Charlton. In fact, as play went on, Ball and Bobby Charlton were seen to be forming part of the 4-3-3 formation. The victory in Madrid sparked off renewed optimism, but a 1-1 draw against Poland (who would torment Ramsey in 1973) at Goodison Park seemed to give the lie to those who claimed that, at last, England had found the right blend.

But once again Ramsey's men confounded their critics as they went to Hampden Park in the April and staged a 4-3 victory, with Hunt, Hurst and Bobby Charlton scoring as the Scots were beaten by the odd goal in seven. Hunt, a two-goal man, was now joining Ball and Charlton as a likely member of the World Cup side, while still there was a query over the name of Greaves. Many saw him as the goal-poacher supreme, others claimed his work rate left something to be desired. Those who saw in Hunt a likely replacement were countered by those who reckoned the Liverpool man was really a willing workhorse. At any rate, England continued to progress, as they went to Wembley and beat Yugoslavia 2-0 in an impressive display. Wingers Paine and Bobby Tambling starred, as did Greaves; and even at that stage, Ramsey was still sorting out what he was going to do – or not do – about genuine wingers. When he took his team on tour before the World Cup began, he also took Ian Callaghan, as well as Paine and Connelly. But Thompson learned that he would not be travelling.

Hunter was seemingly in the England fold, though – he took the place of Moore for the matches against Yugoslavia and Finland (the West Ham man had been in dispute with his club and, indeed, had lost the captaincy). The Finns went down 3-0, but it was not a dashing performance by England … then they came good against Norway as they rattled in half a dozen goals. Four of them came from the mercurial Greaves (he had missed the match against Finland). In time, it was learned that the England sharp-shooter had been adversely affected by a bout of jaundice which took the edge off his play for the best part of a year. This was not realized when, against Denmark, Greaves appeared to be somewhat apathetic, even as England scored a 2-0 success.

Now England were coming down to the last match before the World Cup, and it was considered to be a difficult one, against Poland in Katowice. The last stage of the trip seamed endless, as the coach laboured its way across the Polish countryside and, having been to Poland myself before the end of the Iron Curtain era, I can confirm that in those days a visit to Eastern Europe was something of a depressing affair. Everything appeared to be grey and gloomy, and the people themselves seemed to have little, if anything, to smile about. However, England summoned up the will to overcome any obstacles, as Hunt scored the only goal and the team as a whole turned in a display marked by a willingness to chase and harry. Once again Greaves provided ammunition for his critics. By now, the name of Martin Peters had come into the reckoning, and he did well in the match against Poland.

The World Cup team was coming into shape, with the 'wingless wonders' shortly to be hailed as a master-stroke by a master-tactician. Players such as Paine, Callaghan and Connelly were to find themselves expendable, after fleeting appearances in the World Cup proper. It was a fate which also befell Jimmy Greaves. He was out for good, after the group qualifiers; Connelly played in the first World Cup match, Paine in the second, Callaghan in the third. As for Alf Ramsey, by then he was just a few short weeks away from being hailed as the greatest manager of them all.

CHAPTER 5

AS SOMEONE who covered football matches during the 1966 World Cup, I was able to see some of the finest teams in the world – and to witness, also, some of the thrills and spills which occurred. I can recall the rumpus over Nobby Stiles, the sending-off of Antonio Rattin, the battle between Portugal and Brazil and the game which was almost the shock of the tournament, as Portugal went three goals down inside half an hour against the unrated North Koreans whose names were almost unspellable, and certainly virtually impossible to pronounce … as I discovered when trying to telephone the team over to the copy-taker at *The People* newspaper.

Nobby Stiles? – I've known him since his days as at youngster at Manchester United, and as he tried to make the first team on a regular basis, be suffered from problems with his eyesight – so much so that he had to wear contact lenses. For a considerable time he had difficulty adjusting to them, and he mistimed tackles and 'lost' the ball when it was in the air, especially under floodlights. Not surprisingly, some of his efforts to win the ball were less than successful, and when the World Cup came along he found himself in trouble with referees – indeed, there was a clamour by some people for Alf Ramsey to dispense with Nobby as an England player. After the match between England and France, the FIFA disciplinary committee threatened 'serious action', should Stiles fall foul of authority again, and when officials of the Football Association suggested that it night well be politic to omit the Manchester United player, Ramsey showed that he was still the boss. Stiles stayed.

England versus Argentina? – The Rattin affair created more headlines, as did Portugal's battles against Brazil and North Korea. Portugal were said to have employed strong-arm tactics in their game against Brazil, and it cannot be argued that Pelé became the most notable casualty of the World Cup, when it came to injuries … just as Rattin became the biggest name to receive marching orders. But let us start at the beginning, as England took on Uruguay and, according to one of the observers, 'found themselves goal-less and gripped by baffled rage at the inglorious end to this opening of the World Cup at Wembley'. The writer did add that while he had forecast that England might fail to win on their first outing, they could still figure in the final match and carry off the trophy.

Statistics showed that against Uruguay, England forced 16 corners and had 15 attempts on goal. As for the team from South America, they appeared to have just one thought in mind – the avoidance of defeat by the host country. For most of the time they employed a defensive barrier of eight players, and now and again they reinforced this with another couple. At the final whistle, the fans showed their feelings by some derisive cheers, while the Uruguayan players did a dance of delight. They had succeeded in stifling the game and their opponents. Ramsey's men played with great gusto and not a little skill, but Greaves and Bobby Charlton found themselves being marked throughout the 90 minutes. England had control of the game, Uruguay had control of the goalmouth area, when it came to boarding it up.

On the rare occasions that they did sally forth, the South Americans demonstrated that they possessed skill themselves, though they tried their luck on a couple of occasions from 40 yards out. Some of their tackling left much to be desired, and on one occasion the Hungarian referee, Istvan Zsolt, made it clear to Silva that if there should be any more such reckless tackles, then he would be walking towards the dressing-room. Cortes demonstrated the art of bending the ball as he lashed in a fearsome free-kick which swerved across goal from 30 yards out, then when England did get a sight of goal the Uruguayan 'keeper, Mazurkieviez, saved the day ... by getting his chin in the way of a goalbound flick from Connelly. Not long afterwards Connelly was foiled again, as the 'keeper fisted clear when a goal seemed certain.

Greaves got in a header ... just wide; Connelly's header rapped the bar – but in any case, he was ruled offside; and when Greaves crossed dangerously, Jack Charlton had the chance to get in a clear header, only to see the ball beat the defence, then curl inches wide of a gaping goal. And so England had gained a point, while Uruguay had made one. Then it was on to a match against Mexico (who on their previous Wembley appearance, in 1951, had been humiliated 8-0), and after 90 minutes Ramsey's men had chalked up their first victory, with a 2-0 scoreline. Once again, however, the home team's display raised doubts about their ability to go beyond the quarter-final stages. One writer said that 'unless there is a dramatic injection of imagination in midfield and of vigorous initiative in attack, the dreams that have been cherished over three years of preparation are likely to dissolve miserably'. Such a verdict would have done little to offer comfort to the fans.

Mexico were written off as 'pedestrian', a team scarcely worthy of appearing on the World Cup stage; England were said to have 'laboured' against them, though untroubled in defence. Hunt scored one goal, Charlton the other – and Jack's younger brother was just about the only player to earn praise for having brought some excitement to the occasion. The attacking play as a whole was labelled as 'inefficient'. By that time, France had drawn with Mexico and Uruguay had beaten France; then Mexico drew against Uruguay, and France fell to England, who scored a 2-0 victory for the second time in the tournament. It was reported that while England now were heading for 'a quarter-final assault on the ruthless ranks of Argentina', they were 'still seeking the conviction that would make their forwards feared, their challenge a reality'.

They had despatched France from the World Cup, but 'there was little more than a glimmer of promise' from this display, which featured goals from Hunt (from a corner which Jack Charlton headed against an upright, and with a powerful header from a Callaghan cross). Even so, Banks had to perform a few heroics to deny the

French a goal. Argentina, meanwhile, had reached the quarter-finals by beating Spain 2-1, drawing 0-0 with West Germany and beating the Swiss 2-0. At that stage, there was no hint of the drama that was to accompany the clash between the host nation and the men from South America.

Portugal, whom England would meet in the semi-finals, had despatched Hungary, Bulgaria and Brazil in turn, scoring three goals in each game, and I was at Old Trafford and Goodison Park to see the matches and witness Brazil's eight-year reign as world champions come to an end. Against Portugal at Goodison, Brazil had Pelé injured after only 30 minutes, so he was rendered ineffective – although the Portuguese by then had scored twice. Portugal were strong and possessed skill – in Eusebio, Torres and Simoes they had 'the three musketeers of modern times'. Indeed, when they met North Korea, they needed Eusebio's four goals in order to make a desperate comeback which saw them finally triumph, 5-3. No-hopers North Korea had already staged one major upset by their 1-0 defeat of Italy – it was regarded as 'the biggest shock in the World Cup since that day 16 years ago when the United States beat England by the same score at Belo Horizonte, Brazil'.

But to get down to the nitty-gritty ... the quarter-final between England and Argentina at Wembley, where it was said the home side were 'chased for more than half the game by 10 men after the fiasco of Rattin's expulsion'. It was also said that there might even have been some sympathy for the defiant, depleted South American side ... were it not for 'the total cynicism of their disregard for the laws of the game'. Hurst was the man who won the match for England – he was credited with having 'twice the power, twice the running' of Greaves, and 'that priceless ability in the air which brought a precious goal'. Yet while England's defence was praised, and while Ball was given due credit, the midfield was still termed 'terribly inadequate'.

Argentina had a formation which was flexible – at least, until the dismissal of Rattin. In the early stages, England pushed forward and had two or three attempts to break the deadlock. But soon the tempo of the game – and the temperature inside the stadium – was raised as Ball was blatantly tripped and Hurst was flattened. The home fans began to cheer every kick of the ball by England and to boo every kick of the ball by Argentina. Rattin, it was reported, 'shares the Argentine habit of fouling the man who beats him, almost as a reflex action'. Banks was forced to make one fine save, but England dominated when it came to pressure. As for German referee Rudolf Kreitlein, a small, balding man in black, he had not yet made the decision which focussed attention upon him, as well as upon Rattin.

Even before the major incident in the match, Herr Kreitlein had been a busy man as he jotted down the name of one Argentine player after another in his notebook – 'one was reminded of a schoolboy collecting railway-engine numbers', said one report. Nine minutes before half-time, the game exploded and, 'at last, possibly because he had no pages left', the referee ordered Rattin off the field. He had been booked for a foul on Bobby Charlton and, as captain, he objected to a team-mate having been booked. The referee 'abruptly ordered Rattin off ... Rattin, predictably, wouldn't go'. There was a storm of booing, and Rattin's team-mates – and their manager – remonstrated vociferously with Herr Kreitlein, and then with Ken Aston, head of the referees' committee for the tournament.

For the best part of 10 minutes there was the prospect of the game coming to a summary conclusion, as the whole Argentine team threatened to leave the pitch. At long last, however, Rattin did walk, still protesting that he was innocent. And so half-time arrived, with the game still scoreless. Four minutes into the second half, England were on their way to victory – or so it seemed, until 'keeper Roma pulled off the save of the match as he jack-knifed to turn round a post a point-blank drive from Hurst. It was unlucky 13 – 13 minutes from the end – for Argentina when they finally conceded the goal that won the game, although it came in spectacular style. The ball was moved down the left, from Wilson to Peters, who delivered a dangerous cross, and this time Roma had no chance as Hurst soared to head the ball past him.

Referee Kreitlein said of the Rattin affair that he had taken the player's name once and, the second time around, he had issued a caution. 'He said nothing I could understand, but I could read in his face what he was saying. He was following me around the field shouting at me, but although he towered over me, I was not afraid of him. I had no alternative but to send him off'. Alf Ramsey had something to say, too... 'We still have to produce our best football. It will come against a team who come out to play football and and not act like animals'. His words brought censure from the disciplinary committee of FIFA, in an official letter to the Football Association. There was a broadside, too, from FIFA for the players and officials of Argentina. Whatever the rights and wrongs of the affair, the result stood, and this meant England must meet Portugal in their semi-final match. It was one which, as the Charlton brothers' mother, Cissie, told me later, 'should have been the final'.

If the battle with Argentina had been one which brought little glory, the semi-final was one which was acclaimed not only for the football the fans witnessed, but for its sporting characteristics. It was, said one report, 'as satisfying and sporting as any ever seen on an international field'. England's defence worked hard to shackle the Portuguese attack and, in a game of three goals, two came from Bobby Charlton in genuine style ... 'two typical goals of class'. When Portugal scored from the penalty spot, inside the last 10 minutes, that was the first goal England had conceded in the tournament. It was recorded that this World Cup 'has been marred by chauvenistic dissension, nastiness and ill-feeling'; yet in this match there was not one foul until almost half an hour had gone, and as Portugal flung everything into attack, with Eusebio, Torres and Simoes failing to breach a magnificent England defence, the game ebbed and flowed.

Portugal's defence did not match their attack, and Bobby Charlton found he had room to spare as he worked in a midfield role, spraying passes for strikers Hunt and Hurst to latch on to. Charlton 'capped a memorable night with two such shots as only the complete player can hit, to make two historic goals'. Early on, it was Portugal who made the running; then Hunt and Hurst caused problems for the opposing defence as they chased long balls through the middle. With half an hour gone, Wilson drove the ball forward and Hunt tried to control it; yet though he didn't manage this, Portugal's goalkeeper seemed to panic and he raced out, slid for a yard or so, then appeared to prod the ball away with the sole of his boot. The ball fell for Charlton to clip it straight back into the middle of the empty goal.

Portugal reacted by driving forward, and Banks was grateful to see a drive from Torres scrape past a post and fortunate when a blistering shot from Eusebio squirmed from his grasp but didn't cross the line. Captain Coluna, too, reinforced the attack as he went very close with a fierce drive, and in the second half he ran the midfield for Portugal, while Simoes sparked off attacks and Eusebio went on the prowl to add to his already considerable World Cup tally of goals. But they couldn't break down the rock-like defence of Jack Charlton, Moore and Stiles, even though the giant Torres won more than a few aerial duels. With 20 minutes to go, it was clear that Portugal were beginning to lose heart, and their suspect defence lost another goal.

It was Hurst who broke clear, down the right, and with Bobby Charlton racing through the middle, Hurst delivered a telling pass which his team-mate took in his stride. Charlton barely paused as he despatched a drive goalwards, and the ball sped past the 'keeper and into the net. By then, the home supporters were scenting success, but it wasn't quite 'all over' ... when Torres leaped like a salmon to nod the ball to the unmarked Eusebio, Jack Charlton got there first and punched clear, to concede a penalty. Up strode the dusky Eusebio, and as he struck from the spot he claimed another goal. By now there were fewer than eight minutes to go, and even then Portugal hadn't shot their bolt. Up came Coluna, to rifle a sizzling shot on target; somehow, Banks got to the ball and tipped it over the bar. That really did mark the end of Portugal's efforts to salvage an equaliser. England were through to the final, and destined to meet West Germany, who had hammered five goals past Switzerland in their opening game, drawn 0-0 against Argentina and beaten Spain 2-1 to go through to the quarter-finals. They then scored four times without reply in the match against Uruguay and twice against Russia, at Goodison Park, to earn the right to meet England at Wembley in the 32nd match of the tournament, on Saturday, July 30, 1966.

CHAPTER 6

THE GREATEST day in England's footballing history occurred in front of 96,924 spectators at Wembley stadium, and the receipts of £204,805 were a record for any football match. The scoreline says that in the 1966 final of the World Cup, England defeated West Germany 4-2, in extra time. The scoreline goes nowhere near to illustrating the drama of a match which had seemed to be won – and then had to be won all over again. West Germany had hit an equaliser with almost the last kick of the normal 90 minutes, and in extra time they had almost repeated their escape act ... that was when England struck back to demonstrate that if the match wasn't all over before, it most certainly was now. Because Hurst then made sure the World Cup would be won by England as he delivered the third of his goals, to become the first player to hit a hat-trick in a World Cup final.

This was the player, who little more than a month previously, had seemed to have only an outside chance of appearing on the World Cup stage. Now, instead of Jimmy Greaves, that goal-poacher supreme, it was the West Ham team-mate of Bobby Moore and Martin Peters who held centre stage, after a game which had fluctuated and, seemingly, gone tantalisingly out of England's reach. Yet if Hurst the hat-trick hero was the player who was mobbed, the overall triumph could be set down to England's manager, Alf Ramsey – the man who, boldly (and, some thought, foolishly), had predicted that his team could and would win the Jules Rimet trophy. It was an afternoon which had been charged with emotion from the moment the band of the Royal Marines struck up first chords of the national anthem ... and, in honour of West Germany, Deutschland uber Alles.

It was England who took the initiative at the start, West Germany who seemed the more hesitant; and when Bobby Charlton drove one effort goalwards, 'keeper Tilkowski, challenged by Hurst, knocked himself out as he went to punch clear. Moore put the ball into the net, but the whistle had already gone. Having recovered from that mishap, Tilkowski was called upon to turn a shot from Peters round a post and when Hurst met the corner kick from Ball, he shot over the bar. Then Peters drove a 25-yarder a couple of feet wide ... yet, after all this attacking, England fell behind in the unlucky (for them) 13th minute, as Siggi Held crossed from the left and Wilson, though not under pressure, directed a downward header straight into Haller's path. From a dozen yards, Haller had time and space as he turned and hammered a daisy-cutting right-footer past Banks.

However, six minutes later it was the turn of England fans to raise their voices, as Overath fouled Moore and was penalized. Moore picked himself up, took the free-kick and – from fully 40 yards – steered the ball towards the far post, while Hurst slipped through the defence to meet the ball and head it just inside the post. Tilkowski then snatched a Bobby Charlton effort to safety, at the second attempt, and Banks just beat Haller in a race for possession at the other end. The fans were getting value for their money, and another England goal seemed certain when Hurst, rising to the occasion once more, headed in an effort which Tilkowski could only scramble away. As Ball whipped the ball back into the goalmouth, it was Overath who saved the day with a last-ditch clearance.

When Ball and Cohen failed to take the ball from Held, Jack Charlton came to the rescue, though the tackle cost England a corner – and almost a goal. Overath gained possession, 20 yards out, and he sent in a fierce, rising drive which Banks beat out – only for Lother Emmerich to hammer it straight back. But this time Banks gathered the ball safely. In England's next attack, a Wilson-Hurst move was rounded off by Hunt, but Tilkowski got in the way of the volley; then it was West Germany's turn again, as Overath forced a briliant save from Banks. And so the first half ended in stalemate, with the fans buzzing with excitement and wondering; who would score another goal. They got their answer when, with the match down to its last 15 minutes, they were beginning to think about extra time…

The move began via Hunt and Ball, whose drive was palmed away for a corner by Tilkowski. As the ball came across from the flag-kick, Hurst sent in a shot which Schulz deflected across the face of the goal … leaving Peters to complete the job as he moved in swiftly, unmarked by the defence. The West Ham man hit the ball on the half-volley and, from less than six yards, he could hardly miss. There was danger for England, as Stiles conceded a free-kick, but though the pass from Emmerich beat the defence, when Weber got his head to the ball he could do no better than send in a weak header which, in any event, was off the target. However, as the final seconds of the 90 minutes ticked away, West Germany got out of gaol. A dubious free-kick was given against Jack Charlton, as he leaped to head clear, and from the dead-ball situation Emmerich, the man who packed such a deadly shot, drove the ball right through the defensive wall. It flew across the face of goal, appeared to catch Karl-Heinz Schnellinger on the arm … and (as the referee apparently saw nothing wrong) when the ball reached Weber by the far post, he finished off with a powerful shot. For England, this was a real sickener.

It was recorded that 'rightful victory had been dashed from their grasp, cruelly – indeed, illegally – only seconds from the final whistle'. It was also recorded how Ramsey rallied his men as he told them: 'You've won it once … now win it again'. And when extra time began, his troops raised their game once more, with Ball having a drive tipped over the bar and Bobby Charlton hitting a post. Then, 10 minutes into the extra period, Stiles moved the ball on to Ball, and as he drove in a cross Hurst was there to hammer the ball goalwards. It struck the bar, with Tilkowski beaten, bounced down and came out again – so for agonizing seconds the spectators wondered … would this one count? – Roger Hunt had no doubts; having been up with the action, immediately he turned away to signal a goal; and the referee, Gottfried Dienst, having spoken to his Russian linesman, Bakhramov, confirmed that the goal would stand. It seemed as if this goal would be the winner – and a talking point long afterwards – but England hadn't quite finished, and in a way it was probably a good job that they had one more shot left in their locker, because that way they finished as undisputed world champions.

By this time, both teams had run each other – and themselves – ragged, and players had rolled their socks down as the testing Wembley turf took its toll of tired legs. England tried to keep possession, while the Germans tried to get into the game once more. Wilson took a blow on the head which left him reeling, and as the minutes ticked away with tantalising slowness, the England supporters began to urge the referee to signal the end of play. Then Moore kick-started the move which did indeed confirm that for West Germany, there would be no way back. He delivered a lofted pass into the path of Hurst, who dragged his weary legs across the turf and took the ball with him. Summoning up one final effort, the striker belted the ball into the roof of the net, and with this kick he had become the first player to hit a hat-trick in a World Cup final, while England had triumphed in the first final to go into extra time since 1934, when Italy had beaten the Czechs in Rome.

Of Ramsey, it was said: 'A manager who can instil this kind of spirit in a team, can bring them to this level of fitness, can endow them with so concrete a defence, so persistent an attack, deserves the highest possible credit'. And he received the credit which was his due, as he became Sir Alf Ramsey. 'The England team's triumph is inseparable from his own…' So England – manager, players and supporters throughout the land – celebrated a glorious victory which, sadly was to become the first, and the last, in the next three decades as England's footballing fortunes fluctuated and faded, as hope to turned to despair, and as Ramsey, the architect of his team's finest hour, ended up being given the sack. That sad ending to a distinguished career at international level came eight years after the day of glory, and it was a match against Poland which proved to be the killer blow.

Naturally, when the 1970 World Cup finals were looming, England were tipped to do well once again, and there were plenty of people prepared to gamble that they would retain the trophy, even though they had to travel to Mexico for the finals. Between 1966 and 1970 Ramsey's team played 34 international matches and won a score of them, losing no more than four games. One of those defeats came in a friendly match against West Germany, in Hanover – the Germans' first success against England. Up to then, the best result they had achieved was a 3-3 draw in Berlin, away back in 1930.

There were suggestions that the players available to Ramsey in 1970 were better even than those who had won the World Cup in 1966, and among them were half a dozen of West Germany's conquerors … Banks, Moore, Ball, Bobby Charlton, Hurst, Peters. Yet while England were among the favourites to take the Jules Rimet trophy, some people seemed to forget one thing – that when it came to succeeding in South America, not one European side had ever gone up for the world's most-prized footballing cup. The England squad made a record, before they departed for foreign climes; it was called 'Back Home', and it had a rousing tune and words – so much so that it captured popular imagination and shot to the top of the hit parade. Before long, however, Ramsey and his men were to become involved in various problems, notably the Bobby Moore affair, when he was arrested and alleged to have stolen some jewellery from a hotel shop in Bogota. Eventually, he was cleared, and he went on to give impressive displays on the field of action, but while it lasted, the whole business left a sour taste and did nothing to improve relations with those who were not supporters of England.

Some of Ramsey's statements were regarded as indiscretions – for example, his criticism of the pitch at Guadalajara. And he won few friends among the Latin American media and fans. The actions of Brazil, in contrast, provided food for thought, as they made available free seats for Mexican youngsters and, along with other countries, spent time posing for photographs and providing such extras as souvenir rosettes and paper hats to make it a kind of carnival time, as well as a World Cup footballing occasion. When it came to the games themselves, England did not provide anything in the way of spectacular action; they were professional in the manner in which they did their job, without ever raising spectators to any great level of excitement. Hurst scored the goal against the Rumanians which ensured two points, but when it came to the match against Brazil, the result went the other way round. Not that Ramsey's team was disgraced, far from it. And his players had had to endure a war of nerves – and sound – on the very eve of the game, because raucous fans gathered round the England team's hotel and gave vent to a cacophony of sound as they disturbed the players' slumber. As for the match, that was played in temperatures which reached the high 90's, around noon, and in these conditions the weight rolled off players … half a stone, in some instances.

As had happened back in 1966, when England were scraping results along the way to a glorious finale, there was a crucial lack of scoring power in 1970, and in the final group match, against Czechoslovakia, England had to rely upon a penalty goal from Allan Clarke to squeeze through and emerge second to Brazil, who had hammered the Czechs 4-1 and beaten Rumania 3-2. The Czechs suffered the fate of failing to take even a point from any of their three matches, because they also lost, 2-1, against Rumania. So it was Brazil on six points, England second on four points, Rumania on two points and Czechoslovakia without a point to their name. In another group, West Germany had been taking on Peru, Bulgaria and Morocco – and achieving results similar to Brazil, in that they finished at the top with half a dozen points.

They beat Morocco 2-1, Peru 3-1 and Bulgaria 5-2. So it was Peru, with four points, who accompanied West Germany into the quarter-finals.

There, it was Uruguay against Russia, Italy against Mexico, Brazil against Peru ... and England against West Germany. Russia went out, beaten 1-0; Mexico, the host nation, went out, defeated 4-1; Peru went out, beaten 4-2; and England went out, after having seemingly clinched a place in the semi-finals as they forged a two-goal lead. It us a match which caused considerable controversy, not least when it came to the little matter (or, rather, the very important matter) of substitutions. The quarter-final was played in Leon, and in Gerd Mueller, West Germany had the hit-man of the tournament – hit-man, in the sense of scoring goals. West Germany also had a point to make, in that they were determined to avenge their 1966 defeat at Wembley; but when they went two goals down, you would have put your sweat-stained shirt on England.

The match had always promised to be a classic, and it turned out to be one. England took the game by the scruff of the neck, and when Alan Mullery, and Martin Peters struck, with no more than 20 minutes to go, it looked all over, bar the shouting. However, the West Germans, inspired by 'Kaiser' Franz Beckenbauer, had not quite shot their bolt, and with Beckenbauer gaining control of the midfield play, he finally broke through the England defence to beat stand-in 'keeper Peter Bonetti, who had been pitched in when Banks had had to cry off with a stomach-bug complaint. Now it was 2-1, and the Germans had been given a real incentive to salvage a draw.

It was at this stage that Ramsey took the decision to pull off Bobby Charlton and send on Colin Bell, whose stamina would stand the team in good stead during those final, vital minutes. Ramsey also pulled off Peters and replaced him with the defensive Norman Hunter, and this way, it seemed, England would be able to seal off all routes to their goal. However, West Germany were not to be dismissed from the fray, even at such a late stage, and with Beckenbauer and Overath pulling the strings they surged forward once more ... at which point Uwe Seeler was the man who did the damage, as he scored the goal which took the match into extra time. Shades of 1966 at Wembley! During the extra period, it was Beckenbauer and Overath whose efforts paved the way for yet another German goal – very much an opportunist effort, and typical of the scorer, Gerd Mueller. There simply wasn't time for England to get back into it, and so they had to stage the retreat from Mexico.

It was a retreat which, for Banks, was made all the more unhappy, because back at the team's hotel, he had been watching the match on television, and the transmission was delayed to the point where his England team-mates had arrived back before Banks knew the result. Indeed, even as they returned and he was watching, the game was still at the stage where England were 2-0 ahead, so he was thinking that he would be playing in the semi-finals ... until he realised that his team-mates were not looking downcast just to take the mickey out of him ... they had indeed been defeated.

They had only an academic interest in what happened after that, though the record books show that Italy beat West Germany by the odd goal in seven while Brazil accounted for Uruguay with a 3-1 win and in the final itself, the Brazilians buried Italy as they won 4-1.

At one stage, Ramsey had been quoted as saying that 'we have nothing to learn from Brazil' and, in a sense, this was true – because everyone knew full well just what an accomplished outfit they were, as they demonstrated against Italy in the final. Some people took it as meaning that England's manager didn't believe Brazil could teach us anything, but the words themselves could hardly have been meant in a disparaging fashion. Whatever, between 1970 and 1972 hope began to spring eternal once more, as England started to get results – eight victories and two draws from the 10 matches they played.

Come 1972, and there was the European Nations Cup; and two years after that there would be the World Cup again. In April, 1972, with the European finals looming, West Germany did serious damage to the hopes of England supporters as they went to Wembley and won 3-1. The critics of Ramsey – Brian Clough and Malcolm Allison among them – were ready to have their say. In their group, England beat Malta 1-0 away and 5-0 on home soil; they defeated Greece 3-0 (at home) and 2-0; they won 3-2 in Switzerland and drew the home game 1-1 … then came that 3-1 reverse by West Germany in the quarter-final match with a 0-0 scoreline in the away leg. The Germans marched into the final on the back of a 2-1 win over Belgium in Antwerp, and in Brussels they took the trophy by beating Russia 3-0.

All of which left Ramsey and England looking towards 1974 and the World Cup, which was to be contested in West Germany. Like England (or so we hoped), the Scots would be there – indeed, they were to return home – having finished third in their group, yet not having lost one match. They beat Zaire, drew against Brazil and Yugoslavia. As for England, they never did make it all the way to the finals, as Poland proved to be the stumbling-block upon which our hopes foundered. In England's group for the qualifying matches were Poland and Wales, and it seemed as if these two countries would not pose too much of a threat to Ramsey's ambitions. But the Welsh managed to pull off a draw against England, and when Ramsey took his team to Katowice, the result there was a 2-0 reverse … which left England just one game away from failure to qualify for the finals in West Germany.

Even at that stage, there remained optimism that it wouldn't – couldn't – all go wrong on the night. England lifted their supporters' spirits with a devastating, 5-0 demolition job on the Scots at Hampden Park and a 7-0 hammering of Austria. But the real crunch match was played out on an October night at Wembley stadium, as Poland put the finishing touch to England's dreams. The Polish goalkeeper whom Brian Clough had labelled 'a clown' used just about every part of his body to block England shots and headers, while his team-mates also played their part – none more than Domarski, whose goal just inside the hour really upset the applecart. England did manage an equalizer, from Allan Clarke's spot-kick, but that was it.

Poland went through to the finals of the tournament (they finished at the top of a group which included Argentina and Italy), and they were in the play-off for third place (they beat Brazil by the only goal). England? – They suffered yet again as Italy registered their first-ever victory on English soil, just a month after that demoralising affair against the Poles. And so the writing was on the wall, as the critics went to town and the Football Association pondered not only the loss of prestige, but the loss of revenue that failure to reach the finals of the World Cup must mean. In mid-February, 1974, a committee was formed to consider the future of football, in so far as it affected England, and during the next couple of months there was endless speculation as to where Alf Ramsey would stand. For his part, he made it clear that in some respects he was trying to perform an impossible task.

He offered the Football Association a blueprint which suggested that the England players should have three days in which to prepare for matches and that for European and World Cup qualifiers they should have a week together. There was even a suggestion that England should be involved in an international match each month throughout the course of a season. It mattered not; when the verdict was delivered on April 19, Sir Andrew Stephen, the chairman of the Football Association, and secretary Ted Croker informed Sir Alf that his services were being dispensed with – in other words, he was being sacked. Ramsey was to term it 'the most devastating half-hour of my life.' He said he felt as if he were on trial and that 'I was never given a reason for the sack'. He did not seem too happy, either, about the £15,000 golden handshake after his years of service. Later, he had a brief flirtation with management at club level again – with Birmingham City, where he also became a director – but after five months back in the hot seat, he decided to bow out of management. That was in the spring of 1978.

CHAPTER 7

IN a manner of speaking, Joe Mercer was something like the Dutch boy who stuck his finger in the dyke. He was called upon to get the England show back on the road, after Ramsey's exit and the 1974 failure to qualify for the World Cup. As a player, Mercer had spent 15 years with Everton, where he was regarded almost as an institution – until he was transferred to Arsenal. Having won a League-championship medal with Everton, he went on to spend nine more years at the top with Arsenal, whom he captained in two FA Cup finals (one of them to victory) and to two First Division titles. He also captained his country, as he played 27 times for England and, in 1950, he was elected Footballer of the Year.

Not that Joe Mercer's career was one of unbroken or unparalleled success. A broken leg hastened his retirement as a player – at the age of 40 – and then he took up the challenge of management, first with Sheffield United, then at Aston Villa, where he stayed until the summer of 1964. At one stage he seemed to be everybody's tip to return to Highbury as Arsenal's manager – indeed, almost daily the papers were saying that this event was likely to come to pass, and very soon at that. I knew differently, because I was keeping a close watch on that particular situation, and the information I kept getting was that Joe would NOT become the manager of Arsenal.

I never did discover the hows or the whys of it, but what I did know was that Joe himself was adamant that all the speculation was wide of the mark. This was what he consistently told a close friend and contact who was working for the same newspaper as myself. Remarkably, even though he kept getting this information, the other papers were so strongly supporting the 'Mercer for Arsenal' theme that we doubted the accuracy of what we were being told … yes, even though our own source was constantly double-checking and, each time getting the same feedback from Joe himself. But he never did become the manager of Arsenal, and so all the newspapers turned out to have been wrong.

Joe, who was born in Ellesmere Port and had joined Everton as an amateur in 1930 – he turned professional two years later – was signed by Arsenal in 1946, retired as a player in 1955, and after his stint as manager of Sheffield United he was appointed Aston Villa's team boss in 1959. He remained at Villa Park until the summer of 1964, and by the mid-1960's had done a stint as manager of the England Under-23 side. It was after football, as he told me, had drained him to such an extent that he was suffering from nervous exhaustion, that he learned to pace himself and, from then on, he was ever ready to counsel people to 'make haste slowly'. When he returned to management, with Manchester City, he and his right-hand man, Malcolm Allison, steered the Maine Road club to success as City claimed promotion, the First Division

Joe Mercer, England's caretaker manager for seven games

championship, the F.A. Cup, the League Cup and a trophy in Europe.

No-one could doubt the rich store of knowledge Joe Mercer – 'Uncle Joe', as so many people referred to him – had gained during his career inside football; nor could those who knew him doubt the wisdom he had acquired from the months which he spent outside the game, as he was striving to make a complete recovery from the state of nervous exhaustion to which football – 'my very lifeblood', as he told me – had driven him. And certainly he was able to put all his knowledge to good use when the Football Association turned to him after the departure of Sir Alf Ramsey. It was never going to be a long-term appointment, but the Football Association was hoping 'Uncle Joe' would be able to 'look after the shop' until the right man was found to succeed him.

During the Mercer era, England played seven matches, losing only once; they won three of those games, and when Mercer handed over the reins, he was given a vote of thanks. It was then the turn of another personality who had once been at Manchester City to try his luck ... and Don Revie by that time had made his mark in no uncertain fashion as the team boss of Leeds United. His spell as the manager of England was to last from 1974 to 1977, and to end abruptly and in controversial manner. During his time as the 'gaffer' at Elland Road and, indeed, as a player with Manchester City, he had been the subject of controversy, because some of the things he and his team did gained less than universal approval. Yet almost everyone considered him to be the right man to take charge of England.

Revie was born in Middlesbrough on July 10, 1927, in a terraced house in Bell Street, which was not far from Ayresome Park. His mother died when he was still young, and as he waited for school to start he occupied himself by kicking a ball around. Like Bob Paisley, he had a spell when he became a bricklayer, but as he progressed at football so he moved into the sphere which he had always sought. His first club was Leicester City, whose manager was Johnny Duncan, and he married Duncan's niece, Elsie, who was to be one of his staunchest supporters and a great influence through the remainder of his life. Duncan, too, proved to be a key figure in Revie's days as a player, while Revie repaid the manager's faith in him as he helped Leicester City reach the FA Cup final in 1949 – notably by scoring twice in the 3-1 shock victory over Portsmouth.

However, Revie received a nose injury which came close to costing him his life, for he suffered from a haemorrhage which could scarcely be staunched. Every time he thought he had overcome the problem, the nose would start to bleed again, and he finished up in hospital … and out of the Cup final (which Leicester lost). Having married Elsie Duncan, Revie decided that a transfer would be best, so that nobody could accuse the manager of favouritism if he kept on picking Revie for the team, and it was agreed that he could go. Arsenal wanted him, so did Manchester City; but he settled for Second Division Hull City, where the great Raich Carter was player-manager. Carter saw in Revie his eventual successor. Yet once more Revie decided the time had come for him to be on his travels, and on this occasion he didn't turn down Manchester City.

He did pause to reflect what might have happened, had he said 'Yes' to Tom Whittaker at Arsenal, but as it was he achieved great success with City, although at first it seemed as if he might have made the wrong move. City's manager, a dour Scot named Les McDowall, decided to use a formation which relied upon a deep-lying centre-forward, and he chose Revie to carry out this task. Revie had played other roles in the team, but the plan he was asked to carry out had been tried with some success in the reserves, with Johnny Williamson doing the job. On the first occasion the plan was tried out in the senior side, City came unstuck as Preston hit them with five goals at Deepdale – but in the next game, City themselves hit Sheffield United with a nap hand of goals. For that match, wing-half Ken Barnes came into the side, and he and Revie hit it off from the start. As a result, what became known as The Revie Plan also became the talk of football, not least when Manchester City ended up by going to Wembley.

However, they lost the 1955 final against Newcastle United, although they vowed that they would be back 12 months later ... and they were, with Revie this time helping them to beat Birmingham City. As Revie himself acknowledged, the deep-lying centre-forward plan had been adapted from the Hungarian style of play when they were at the top of the international tree and had Bozsik and Hidegkuti in their ranks. According to Revie, Barnes played the Bozsik role, as he supplied the passes for Hidegkuti, although, of course, at City Barnes was the 'feed' man for Revie. So the attacking wing-half combined with the deep-lying centre-forward ... and it was up to the opposition to try to fathom things out. Although City finished as Wembley losers in 1955, for Revie the season was a personal triumph, because he took the Footballer-of-the-Year award, and along with his winner's medal in the FA Cup in 1956, he finished up with half a dozen appearances for England to his credit.

There came a time during his days at Maine Road when he was in dispute with the club, and for a brief while he even trained on his own. Some people treated him as Revie the rebel, while others were on his side. Eventually, he signed for Sunderland, and after a two-year spell there he arrived at Leeds United, who paid £14,000 for him. That was in 1958, by which time the transfer fees paid for him in total were a record for that era in the game. Revie was to repay Leeds over and over again for their outlay.

It may not have seemed that way as (just a year after Revie's arrival) Leeds slid down to the Second Division; then they looked like slipping down to the Third. Leeds gave Revie a vote of confidence, however, by making him their manager and, in partnership, with chairman Harry Reynolds, he began the battle to revive club fortunes. I knew Reynolds, a blunt Yorkshireman who had plenty of 'brass' – though he carried his cigarettes in a battered old tin. He used to say: 'You get nowt for being second'. And he didn't intend Leeds to be second-best, either. Perhaps Revie's most crucial signing was Bobby Collins, the Scotland international. Leeds paid Everton £25,000 – and more than got their money back. I knew Bobby well; indeed, when he learned he was up for sale, he rang me to say Leeds were in for him. I advised him to hang on and see who else showed interest. Bobby stayed the night at my house, travelled to Leeds next day – and rang me to say: 'I've signed'. I told him: 'You bloody fool!' But he and Revie had the last laugh, because the move turned out to be great for both men.

It's history now how Leeds went up to the First Division, went to Wembley in 1965, won trophies at home and abroad ... even if they did have their staggering failures, as well (their 1970 FA Cup-final-replay defeat by Chelsea; a 3-2 FA Cup defeat by Fourth Division Colchester United in season 1970-71; their Wembley defeat by Second Division Sunderland in 1973). Overall, however, the picture of Revie as manager of Leeds United is one of great success – even if he and his players were hurt by accusations that they would do almost anything to win, once they got out on the park. Revie himself had been a fighter, as a player, as well as a rebel; he had suffered a badly-fractured ankle (it was broken in three places) and been warned that he might never kick a ball again – 'the doctors say it's 1,000 to one against you'. Revie was just 19 then – and 19 weeks later he was back in action, for Leicester City reserves. As the manager of Leeds, he was ready to battle to achieve success, and while the tag of 'dirty Leeds' certainly took some time to live down, eventually the world of football did come to acknowledge that Revie's team, in its all-white strip, was gifted with tremendous talent, as well as containing players who were not reluctant to make crunching tackles when the going got rough.

There were even stories to the effect that Leeds had sought to influence the result of a crucial match – allegations always denied by Revie – and on one occasion a referee reported Revie to the Football Association for having, in his opinion, spoken publicly out of turn about another referee. Among some vitriolic comments about Leeds United was one suggestion from Brian Clough, then the manager of Derby County, that Leeds should be made to suffer relegation – was that tongue-in-cheek, or serious? – Clough himself lived to rue the brief time (44 days) he spent at Elland Road as manager of Leeds United. One way and another, during the Revie era Leeds United's name was on most people's lips week in, week out, as they powered their way to trophies, for the most part, and faltered and failed on some surprising occasions.

When Leeds had gone through an entire season with only two defeats and taken the championship with a total of 67 points, I discussed this tremendous feat with Revie, and he told me: 'I think that one day some club may just total more points than we've done, but I doubt if anyone will suffer fewer defeats'. It took Bob Paisley's Liverpool to eclipse that Leeds record when they finished with 68 points. Revie had changed his team's strip to the all-white of Real Madrid, and he had visions of emulating the crack Spanish club by winning the European Cup. Had he stayed at Elland Road, the dream might have been realised … but a telephone call changed the course of his career and, indeed, his life. The Football Association had parted company with Sir Alf Ramsey, and the England job was up for grabs.

Three names were seemingly in the frame – those of Gordon Milne, Jimmy Bloomfield and Gordon Jago – but when Revie rang Ted Croker, the secretary of the Football Association, it seemed there was no further need to consider options. Revie's record as a player and as a manager spoke volumes. He had played for his country, he had managed a club which had succeeded at home and abroad, setting records along the way. At that stage, few people were ready to express their opposition to the appointment of Don Revie – although there was one noted old adversary in Alan Hardaker, secretary of the Football League. From many discussions with Alan, I knew that he was not a lover of the man who managed Leeds United, although he could acknowledge the success he had achieved.

Hardaker had a soft spot for Joe Mercer, who had steered England through a successful summer tour of Europe; and in fairness to Revie, Alan admitted that here was a man big enough to tackle the job – although he added a proviso that well as possessing the right qualities, Revie also had 'all the faults of the modern manager'. According to Hardaker, who had crossed swords more than once with the Leeds team boss, Revie was 'totally ruthless, selfish, devious and prepared to cut corners to get his own way'. At the same time he was a family man, could be engaging when he wanted to be, was 'acutely aware of his responsibilities and enormously hard-working'. Hardaker bluntly summed up that in his position as secretary of the Football League, when it came to dealing with Don Revie, he found him to be 'a pain in the neck' – and, had he been talking in private, 'neck' was not the word Alan would have used.

Hardaker acknowledged that, like himself, Revie had a job to do; so the pair were often on collision course. According to Hardaker, also, Revie's switch to the international arena was 'a classic example of poacher turning gamekeeper … very quickly after his appointment I discovered that Don now saw things in an entirely new light'. At a meeting with Revie, Ted Croker and Dick Wragg, then the chairman of the international committee, Hardaker, as League secretary, promised Revie, as England manager, 'the same co-operation that he had given Alf Ramsey'. This, of course, was a reference to the club-or-country issue when it came to releasing players for international duty, and while Hardaker recalled that his tongue-in-cheek remark brought smiles all round, one of those smiles was 'perhaps a shade on the frosty side.'

There was the famous story about Revie and Professor Sir Harold Thompson, who – like Hardaker – was a man who spoke plainly. Thompson, born in Sheffield, had once run the old Pegasus side when it had been in its pomp, and his major sphere of influence had been on the amateur side of the game. The story went that shortly after Revie had been named as England's manager, Thompson said to him: 'When I get to know you better, Revie, I shall call you Don'. To which Revie was said to have retorted: 'And when I get to know you better, Thompson, I shall call you Sir Harold'.

Sir Harold and Don Revie were later to become involved in an acrimonious court battle, after the latter's defection to the United Arab Emirates had brought about a Football Association verdict that he had brought the game into disrepute. However, at the beginning all appeared to be sweetness and light, even if Leeds United did accept Revie's resignation with extreme reluctance – indeed, there was talk at the time of Leeds seeking compensation from the Football Association for the loss of their manager, much as they must concede that he was being asked to succeed in a higher calling. The Football Association, faced with the suggestion that it should fork out an amount of money greater than any transfer fee previously paid for an English footballer, jibbed – and Leeds subsequently agreed that they would be prepared to accept a contribution towards the appointment of a successor as their manager.

For his part, Revie did not go it alone … he took trainer Les Cocker with him, so the Elland Road club suffered a double blow. But the directors – and the players – acknowledged that no-one could deny Revie the right to try his luck in the nation's most prestigious footballing job. The way he had looked after his team was summed up by Allan Clarke… 'He did everything for us, fathered us, left nothing to chance. Anything we wanted, he'd do for us'. That remark about 'leaving nothing to chance' found an echo in Alan Hardaker's opinion that Revie always wanted to get things done in a manner which would be of benefit to his team – 'unless he could control everything, he seemed to feel the dice were being deliberately loaded against Leeds'.

When Revie kicked off his international career as a manager, just about the first thing he did was to try to get the Football League to agree to postpone Saturday games involving England men, immediately before they were due to play for their country. Hardaker couldn't commit the League but suggested that things might move in that direction at some time in the future. Revie's translation of this was that it had been a firm promise – and Hardaker publicly denied it. From then on, they had a relationship which made both men wary of each other. As for achieving results, Revie soon demonstrated that he intended to do the job his way, as he called up no fewer than 81 players, at various times, experimenting and striving to mould a team which would win match after match. His first year was a successful one, too.

First there was a 3-0 victory over Czechoslovakia, in the European-championship contest, and then (after three players had been omitted) came a 0-0 draw against Portugal. There were more team changes, and in March, 1975, England took on West Germany at Wembley, as the 100th international match was staged. The player who had the honour of leading the team out was Alan Ball, and Revie's side consisted of 11 players from 10 different clubs. Ball led England to their first win over the old enemy since the 1966 World Cup, but Revie was still cautious in his comments. 'There is a lot to do yet', he warned, though he added that 'the foundation is there'. The following month it was the turn of striker Malcolm Macdonald to hit the headlines, as he knocked in all five goals against Cyprus, and victory in the Limassol return seemed to have clinched a place in the European championships – indeed, England had still to concede a goal six months after Revie had taken charge.

England also made certain of emerging as champions in the home-international series as they saw off the Scots with a 5-1 win at Wembley, although there were some mutterings of discontent by one or two players, since the team changes being rung obviously could not satisfy everyone. Kevin Keegan, Ball and Alan Hudson were among those who discovered that they were considered to be expendable, on occasion, but Revie refused to admit that he could be wrong about ringing the changes. His attitude: 'I don't want any players with me in the World Cup who go running for the plane home if they're left out for one match'. He had been offered a friendly word of advice by Alan Hardaker that managing an international side would be different from handling players at club level and, of course, he knew this for himself. In fact, he decided that the players on whom he came to depend, with England, should also feel that they could depend upon him, and he managed to obtain a new pay deal for them. There were incentive payments such as £5,000 for appearing in the finals of the European championships, with a £2,000 bonus for getting to the quarter-finals and another £1,000 a time for success in the semi-finals and the final. Revie countered criticism of this cash deal by saying that while he expected his players to wear their England shirts with pride, their financial rewards should also be in line with the kind of money coming into the Football Association's coffers as a result of the players' efforts.

In the event, the players' efforts didn't produce the expected results as time went by ... the return match against the Czechs, in Bratislava, saw England losing by the odd goal in three and thus the first defeat in nine matches meant that the qualifying group had become rather more open. When Portugal held England to a 1-1 draw the following month, it meant that England had no longer any interest in the European championships, and Revie's reputation was being questioned – not least by those

Don Revie who, after achieving so much success with Leeds United, left the England job under a cloud.

critics who had complained that the players were being distracted by the money motive. Revie, of course, could counter that his players would be losing money by losing matches, so if anything, the money motive should inspire them to even greater efforts. He certainly made the point that some players didn't appreciate how lucky they were to be doing something they loved and, at the same time, to be so well-paid for the job. His verdict reminded me of what a former England captain, Ronnie Clayton, had told me years earlier … that he didn't regard himself as a Soccer slave, but as a slave to Soccer, because he was being paid to do a job he enjoyed doing, anyway.

There were those who ridiculed Revie's dossiers on opposing teams, his carpet-bowls-and-bingo sessions for his players, as he attempted to mould his England squad into a family, just as he had moulded his players at Leeds United. The knives were out in some quarters and, of course, in the final analysis it all depended upon results. England failed to retain the home-international championship in May, 1976, when they fell to the Scots, and there was some pessimism about the prospects for Revie's team when they came up against Italy in the qualifiers for the World Cup. However, a 4-1 victory over Finland in Helsinki temporarily stifled the critics, as England embarked upon the World Cup trail, and with the Wembley return to come, it seemed as if the Finns would suffer a mauling there. As it turned out, England managed to win only by the odd goal in three, and when Italy chalked up a 2-0 success in Rome, the writing was on the wall, because not only must England win the return game, they must also get the scoring ratio right. There were three matches left … home and away against unrated Luxembourg, and the Wembley date with Italy. Revie declared: 'The task is far from impossible; our destiny is in our hands'.

When Holland sent their international side to Wembley for a friendly, they scored a 2-0 victory and left Revie admitting that 'they taught us how far we've got to go'. He compared the Dutch with the Magical Magyars of the 1950's. By this time it seemed he was beginning to think not only in terms of having to battle to reach the World Cup, but of having to face up to the fact that he could be heading for the sack – and it was around this time that he received the first approaches from the United Arab Emirates. Meanwhile, the flak was beginning to build up, and even a 5-0 victory over little Luxembourg did no more than bring momentary relief. The home-international championships, with Scotland winning 2-1 at Wembley, demonstrated how much of a struggle England faced when it came to the World Cup, and Revie himself decided the time had come for action … on his own behalf.

The Italians were taking on Finland in Helsinki, and Revie was reported to be flying out to spy on England's key opponents. However, before he travelled to Finland he had a date in Dubai, there to talk terms with his prospective new bosses. The Football Association knew nothing of this trip at the time, and Revie did go from London to check on Italy when they played the Finns in Helsinki. He saw Italy score a convincing victory, and then it was time for Revie and his players to be or their travels to South America. That tour brought renewed optimism that all was not yet lost, because England emerged undefeated - but it was while Revie was in Buenos Aires that he first acquainted Dick Wragg, chairman of the international committee, of his thoughts about quitting his job. He still had a couple of years to go on his contract, but he argued that if the Football Association paid him off with £50,000 his departure at this stage would be 'in the best interests of the team' – and, of course, it would save the association not only the bother of sacking him in the near future, but of possible action when it came to the cash side of things.

Revie's argument was that while he had not committed himself to the United Arab Emirates, he believed he had done enough to deserve compensation from the Football Association, not least from a public-relations and sponsorship point of view. He had ensured that cash had gone into the association's coffers and, in return, he felt entitled to some compensation. And it could not be denied that the international gates had risen during Revie's spell as England team boss, while sponsorship deals had benefited the Football Association.

It may or may not have come as a shock to Revie that the association decided it was not prepared to play; instead, and especially given the fact that (hopefully) a World Cup campaign was looming, the officials made it plain that the manager retained their confidence. Where they miscalculated was that they didn't believe Revie would defect. It was said that the United Arab Emirates were ready to pay Revie a salary of £60,000, tax-free and excluding bonuses, and in the end the Football Association learned all about it the hard way – via a world exclusive in the *Daily Mail*, as Jeff Powell broke the news that England no longer had a manager. The front-page story broke on July 11, and the world of football was flabbergasted. Revie was revealed as a man torn between wanting to do the best he could for his country, and wanting also to do the best he could for his family.

He revealed that he had sat down one evening with his wife, Elsie, and talked things through. 'We agreed that the job (of managing England) was no longer worth the aggravation. It was bringing too much heartache to those nearest to us. Nearly everyone in the country seems to want me out. So I am giving them what they want. I know people will accuse me of running away, and it does sicken me that I cannot finish the job by taking England to the World Cup finals in Argentina next year. But the situation has become impossible'. Thus the explanation from Don Revie, the man whose action brought instant accusations of dereliction of duty. What made it all the worse, from a Football Association point of view, was that the story broke before Revie's letter of resignation reached the appropriate quarter.

If the knives had been out before, the arrows were now being fired in profusion at the heart of the target, and among the barbs came a wry sentence or two of condemnation from one of Revie's long-time protagonists, Alan Hardaker. Like this:

'Don Revie's decision doesn't surprise me. I can only hope he can quickly learn to call out bingo numbers in Arabic'. The tabloid's began to dig, of course, and bribery allegations were raked up again, with Revie not only making his denials, but threatening court action. This did not materialise from the former England manager, though his one-time skipper at Leeds, Billy Bremner, did win libel damages believed to be in excess of £100,000. For Revie, his defection abroad was damaging in itself.

The Football Association charged him with having brought the game into disrepute, and at a hearing which Revie refused to attend, he was suspended indefinitely from involvement in any football under the association's aegis until he did come forward to face their charges. It was a year later when Revie's legal advisers revealed that he would now be prepared to appear before the commission, so the hearing was set for December 18, 1978. Revie's counsel claimed that the Football Association had no jurisdiction over him; there was, further, an objection to the presence of Professor Sir Harold Thompson as president, on the grounds that as chairman of the Football Association he could not be impartial. When it was all done and dusted, the objections raised by Revie's advisers had been squashed and the verdict delivered ... a 10-year ban from English football.

By November, 1979, Revie was taking his case to the High Court, claiming that the ban was illegal and that he should be awarded damages. Various football personalities were called – Jimmy Hill (giving evidence for Revie), Lawrie McMenemy and Jock Stein (giving evidence as to the precarious business of being a football manager). When it came to Professor Sir Harold Thompson, Revie's counsel described him as having been 'prosecutor, witness, judge and jury'. Having heard the complaints regarding Thompson, the judge, Mr. Justice Cantley, concluded that Revie – 'a very prickly man' – had been 'brooding on imagined wrongs'. Yet the judge also acknowledged the possibility of bias as a result of the FA chairman having presided at the hearing. 'I think he should not have done so, and particulary after the situation was pointed out to him at the hearing, as it was ... In either event, the decision of the commission, with its heavy penalty, cannot stand'. And so the 10-year ban on Revie was thrown out.

Nevertheless, he had to endure words of condemnation from the judge, as he termed the former England team boss 'very greedy' and 'selfish'. According to the judge, Revie 'held the highest post of its kind in English professional football, and he published and presented to the public a sensational and notorious example of disloyalty, breach of duty, discourtesy and selfishness. His conduct brought English professional football, at a high level, into disrepute'. When Revie's barrister suggested his client had been shown little warmth, Mr. Justice Cantley answered: 'I haven't exhibited any more than I can help'.

From a financial point of view, Revie had good cause to be satisfied, since the Football Association was ordered to pay all its own costs and one-third of the former manager's; so the association in total was estimated to have had find the best part of £150,000 – which was a great deal of money close on two decades ago. Almost a decade before that, in fact, Revie had displayed more than a modicum of financial acumen by doing a deal with his club, Leeds United – one which, from New Year's Day, 1980, would bring him over nine years a guaranteed £10,000 a year from consultancy fees. Clearly, he had been looking ahead to the day when he no longer wished to be involved in a job which involved active participation for seven days a week – instead, the consultancy provided for him to attend no more than four board meetings during the course of a year. Now, with the judgment from Mr. Justice Cantley, Revie could call in that contract he had negotiated with his former club, should he so wish. The 10-year ban was a dead duck.

There was a touch of irony about one thing, in connection with England's efforts to reach the finals of the World Cup in Argentina … they did manage to get the better of Italy, although they still failed to qualify on the score of inferior goal difference. But having got thus far, they found the nation's fans were inclined to view matters in a more sympathetic light – possibly, to some extent, because those same fans still looked upon Don Revie with an extreme degree of disfavour, after his abrupt and unheralded departure from the England job. Years later, a former captain of England, Kevin Keegan, was to say he had felt sad that the public generally had retained the wrong impression of a man who was kind, generous and caring. 'When he left the England job he did the right thing for his family, but did it wrongly. He knew it, was big enough to admit it.' Keegan also reckoned that Revie would have enjoyed similar success to Ramsey 'if the players had been good enough'. Keegan's verdict: 'We weren't.'

Revie's jobs abroad after his exit from the England post took in stints with Al Nasr and National FC, Cairo. While he won his battle with the Football Association, he finally lost out in the greatest battle he ever had to face – the fight for life itself. In August, 1987, the news broke that he was suffering from the debilitating motor-neurone disease.

It was sad to see a man who, once, had been the picture of health, sitting in a wheelchair; sad, also, to recall that the disease had struck him down at a time when, under normal circumstances, he should have been able to look forward to days of golf and other such pleasures. His former Leeds players rallied round, as did his friends – and he still retained many who had championed him in the dark days of his exit from these shores. Revie, once he knew what was in store for him, responded as he had done when he was the manager of Leeds. He was ready to fight. 'It's not all doom and gloom', he observed, as he declared also that he intended to make every effort to raise an much money as possible so that further research could be undertaken in the effort to find a cure for motor-neurone disease. One was tempted to wonder if the toll of fighting to clear his name over a lengthy period of time had had anything to do with his contracting the disease.

As I knew well enough, in life he had been a superstitious man, to some degree – that 'lucky' blue suit, for instance. And when he died, on May 28, 1989, it would not have been lost upon him that this was the 80th birthday of Sir Matt Busby (the man to whom at the outset of his managerial career, he had turned for advice). Revie then had said that Busby could have kept all his secrets to himself; instead, he answered every question the new boy put to him, and hid nothing. I always found Don Revie approachable, and we never had a cross word. I felt that, deep down, he was suspicious until he got to know you and feel he could trust you. Certainly, I liked him, even though I still find it strange that he should have brought an illustrious and successful career to such an untimely end in the manner that he did. As Kevin Keegan said, what he did, he did for his family … but, sadly, he did it in the wrong way and at the wrong time.

Ron Greenwood who took over the role of England manager after the acrimonious departure of Don Revie

CHAPTER 8

MENTION the name of Ron Greenwood, and you immediately think of West Ham United, a club which is usually regarded as one of the schools of Soccer science. Few people would associate the name of Greenwood with a northern cotton town where the local football club was ruled for years by a butcher whose name is commemorated by a stand. Yet Ron Greenwood, whose accent might well be termed 'classless' – it certainly isn't broad Lancashire – was born in Burnley, which is not far from the Ribble Valley and the Witches-of-Pendle fame. However, most of Greenwood's career in professional football was spent in the south of England – apart from a spell in Yorkshire (with Bradford Park Avenue), he was a player with Chelsea, Brentford and Fulham.

Greenwood, who was cast in the Walter Winterbottom mould – a Soccer tactician, although perhaps not quite so scholarly – claimed a League-championship medal while with Chelsea (in season 1955-56) and graduated to the status of an England B international. Always interested in the coaching side of Soccer, he gave Oxford University and Walthamstow the benefit of his experience in this direction, and he managed Eastbourne and the England youth team. He became a coach to the England Under-23 side, spent some time as coach and assistant manager at Arsenal, and ended up at the club with which his name is always associated – West Ham. He coached and managed the Hammers from 1961, and for the 1966 and 1970 World Cup tournaments he was a technical adviser to FIFA. Not a bad pedigree with which to emerge as a candidate for the job of managing England, once Don Revie had travelled on to the Middle East. And, of, course, when he was put in charge of the international team, it was at a tricky time.

It was what Professor Sir Harold Thompson, chairman of the Football Association, termed 'a bit of a situation … we need a firm, stable hand immediately'. Thompson was at that moment passing on to Greenwood an invitation to become England's team manager – but on a caretaker basis. They had got together for a chat at a hotel not far distant from the Association's Lancaster Gate headquarters, and Greenwood, then aged 55, was to admit later that he felt he was being sized up for the job largely because he was one of the few men available. With season 1977-78 on the horizon, there could be no question of the Football Association risking accusations of trying to poach a team boss from one of the clubs, but Greenwood, it would appear, was not really seen as more than a stop-gap appointment. Indeed, when the news broke, it was said that he would 'act as team manager for the next three internationals, until December'.

He might have been born up north, he might have played football in clogs as a nipper; but as a player and a coach he had demonstrated his abilities during a career which had seen him steer West Ham to success in the FA Cup and the European Cup-winners Cup. Bobby Moore, Martin Peters and Geoff Hurst had been his protégés, and they had figured prominently in England's World Cup triumph. Greenwood himself, having managed at Upton Park until 1974, had then settled for becoming general manager, with team affairs coming under the control of John Lyall. As it turned out, Greenwood was to rue the day he gave up such close involvement with his players at West Ham – not that Lyall didn't deserve his chance; but the man from Burnley discovered that as time went by he was missing out to such a degree that 'my spirit was low'. He wasn't over-enamoured of the way the game itself was going, either, so he jumped at the opportunity to show the world that England's team 'could still play a bit'. And he was keen 'to help restore faith and dignity in our game'.

Greenwood, like Walter Winterbottom, was a bit of a visionary; but he also knew his football – which, to him, was a game which should be played with skill, as well as endeavour. The man who had landed the job as caretaker manager found himself in charge for another four and a half years, after his initial, three match stint. And between 1977 and 1982, when he bowed out, he took England to the finals of the European championships and of the World Cup.

Greenwood returned to the north of England, for a start – he went to Liverpool to talk to Bob Paisley, the man who had reluctantly taken over from Bill Shankly ... and who had succeeded beyond the wildest dreams of the Anfield club's supporters. Like Greenwood, Paisley had regarded himself as 'a buffer' when handed the job; now, England's caretaker boss was turning to Bob ... and to Liverpool Football Club for its players. Half a dozen men from Anfield were chosen, along with Kevin Keegan (recently moved from Liverpool to SV Hamburg) for the first international under Greenwood's rule. It was a friendly against Switzerland at Wembley, and the new team boss had to settle for a scoreless draw. The next outing was away, against Luxembourg, and for this World Cup qualifier Greenwood picked five Liverpool men. The result was a 2-0 victory, and while this was obviously an improvement upon the result against the Swiss, it didn't depose Italy from their position at the head of the group.

Greenwood decided that the time had come to make a few changes, and so he went outside Liverpool for a couple of wingers and a striker. Manchester United's Steve Coppell – who hailed from Merseyside – and Manchester City's Peter Barnes claimed their first caps, as did the striker – an Everton player by the name of Bob Latchford. Keegan was still there, and two players from London clubs were given their heads in the midfield department. One was Trevor Brooking, from West Ham; the other was Ray Wilkins, from Chelsea. Liverpool? – They were still well represented, because they had three players in the England side – goalkeeper Ray Clemence, right-back Phil Neal, and skipper Emlyn Hughes. They knew each other's style of play well enough, having been together so often as part of Liverpool's defence. And so the stage was set for an audience of 90,000 people at Wembley.

If Don Revie, seemingly, had given up the ghost when it came to taking England to the finals of the World Cup in Argentina in 1978, his defection didn't mean that it was all over bar the shouting ... Italy still had to be met and, hopefully, mastered at Wembley in November, 1977 ... and they were. Keegan supplied the finish to a Brooking-inspired move, then Brooking gave Keegan the credit for having made his goal. The Italians, who had walked out as favourites to win, went back to their dressing room after having lost, 2-0.

However, that success was not quite sufficient to send Greenwood's team on its way to South America, because the Italians went on to defeat Luxembourg 3-0 in Rome and thus have the edge on England by a goal difference of three. Greenwood's three-match reign had come to an end, and the question now was who should be given the chance to take England through to the European championships in 1980. The Football Association settled on a short list of five: Brian Clough, Bobby Robson, Lawrie McMenemy, Allen Wade (the FA's own director of coaching) ... and Ron Greenwood. When the interviews had been conducted the vote was delivered, and Greenwood's name topped the list.

This didn't mean that all the others were being ditched. Greenwood himself wanted backing from coaches and managers, so that there would be continuity, and control of the England B team was handed to Bobby Robson and Don Howe (who had been an Arsenal coach during the year they did the double). When it came to the England Under-21 side, three men were brought into the picture ... Dave Sexton, Terry Venables and Howard Wilkinson. And there was a job of work, as well, for Brian Clough – along with Peter Taylor, he was given charge of the England youth team, with former West Ham footballer John Cartwright as the full-time coach. However, Clough's connection was not to last very long, largely because he had enough on his plate in taking Nottingham Forest towards the championship.

In so many ways, the urbane Greenwood could be considered a success as England's team boss; he was in charge for 55 matches, of which 33 were won and a dozen drawn. England qualified for the European finals and dropped only one point in doing so. They went to Denmark and won 4-3, they did the double with a 1-0 win on home soil. Northern Ireland conceded nine goals in their two games (it was 4-0 at Wembley, 5-1 away). Bulgaria were beaten 3-0 on their own patch and 2-0 in England, which left the Republic of Ireland with the best record of the lot ... they lost 2-0 away, but held England to a 1-1 draw on Irish soil. So England went to the finals, with games to play against Belgium, Italy and Spain. They drew 1-1 with the Belgians, lost 1-0 against Italy and beat Spain 2-1. That was the end, as Italy marched on, along with Belgium, who had beaten Spain and drawn with the Italians.

However, the results did not tell the whole story – far from it, because when England and Belgium met, crowd trouble erupted, as Italian fans in the ground in Turin began to jeer their English counterparts, and almost before anyone realised what was happening, there was an outbreak of fighting behind the England goal. The Italian police swiftly went into action, taking their batons to the feuding fans and firing cannisters of tear-gas into the crowd, as well. As the fans began to feel the effects of the tear-gas, the smoke billowed and drifted in the direction of the England goalmouth, where Ray Clemence soon found himself not only unable to keep his mind on the football, but unable to see what was going on. When the backroom men on the England bench spotted what was happening, as Clemence indicated his plight, Ron Greenwood decided the time had come for action on behalf of his goalkeeper – he asked the match adjudicator to get the referee to halt the proceedings.

There was almost an element of comedy about it as Greenwood asked the West German referee what would be the outcome, should Clemence concede a goal while he was suffering from temporary blindness, because of the smoke in his eyes. The referee replied that the goal would still stand – so Greenwood then put it to the official that the game should be halted; and it was. Five minutes later, play was resumed, but there were no more goals – Ray Wilkins had scored England's, Jan Ceulemans had been Belgium's marksman. The crowd trouble had repercussions for England ... not only did more than 70 spectators require hospital treatment, but UEFA fined the Football Association £8,000, while some Italian sportswriters suggested that England should be summarily dismissed from the tournament. Considering that the gate had been little more than 15,000, it all seemed to have been 'over the top'; and with a 60,000 crowd expected for the match against Italy, there were heavy-handed hints that any English fans who transgressed would be in dire trouble. Italy showed that they were prepared to battle it out on the field of play, and Marco Tardelli's goal ensured their victory. In the third match, goals from Trevor Brooking and Tony Woodcock beat Spain, and when England's participation in the tournament had ended. Greenwood had nothing but praise for the effort his players had put in.

When Italy and Czechoslovakia fought it out for third place, a 1-1 draw was followed by a penalty shoot-out, with the Czechs winning 9-8; and in the final itself, West Germany wound up with a 2-1 victory over Belgium. By which time Ron Greenwood was thinking ahead to the World Cup finals of 1982, and weighing up the opposition along the way. Two nations would qualify from England's group, which included Rumania, Hungary, Norway and Switzerland – and as the games came and went, so did one of the best-kept secrets in football, because England's manager at one stage told his bosses and his players that he was calling it quits. This came about as a result of what he considered to be his own failure to do the job as it should have been done.

England kicked off by beating Norway 4-0 at Wembley, but after that things began to go sadly awry ... the worst run in England's history produced only one win in the next eight matches and – naturally – Greenwood became the target for bitter criticism. Spain, Brazil and Scotland all went to Wembley – and won; England went to Bucharest and were beaten 2-1 by Rumania (who also drew the return, 0-0); and England just managed to beat the Swiss 2-1 at Wembley. Four games had brought only five points, so Spain was beginning to seem a bit of a mirage, with qualifying matches against Switzerland and Hungary – both away – to be played. One newspaper advised Greenwood to 'pack up' ... and things got worse as England not only lost to Switzerland for the first time in more than 30 years, but as their so-called fans got drunk and caused havoc inside the stadium in Basle. The Swiss police confessed that they had never experienced such outrageous behaviour from football followers before.

On top of the 2-1 defeat, the crowd trouble served only to harden the resolve of England's manager, who let his bosses know he intended to retire after the match in Hungary. Greenwood's decision, it was agreed, would remain secret until the team returned from Budapest ... where his players did him proud as they scored a 3-1 victory. Even so, he still intended to go, and his after-match Press conference consisted of just four sentences, one of which was: 'I don't want to answer any questions...' Yet, believe it or not, there wasn't a hint in the papers next day that he was on his way out of football.

It was remarkable, in a game where the slightest sniff of a rumour can produce a back-page story after someone has added two and two and come up with the figure five. Greenwood had simply thanked the sportswriters, termed England's victory well-deserved, and finished up by saying: 'I don't want to answer any questions. Thank you'. He was saving his real statement of intent for the players on the flight back to Luton. There was less than half an hour to go to touch-down when Greenwood faced his players, thanked them all – and delivered the bombshell news that he was going into retirement. Ho told them that Dick Wragg, chairman of the Football Association's international committee, would be making the official announcement once they had landed. Greenwood added that with seven points in the bag and Norway away and Hungary to come at Wembley, he believed England could make it to the finals of the World Cup in Spain, and that his successor, whoever he might be, would have a decent chance of achieving something there.

At first, the players were dumbstruck, then they started to try to persuade Greenwood to change his mind; and even as it seemed they were failing – the appeals were still going on as they walked towards the baggage area at Luton airport – Greenwood was starting to have second thoughts. Dick Wragg was waiting to meet him – and he had already decided to have one last go ... then he learned that, at the final minute, England still had a manager. Astonishingly, even then the story never broke in the papers. Yet as events unfolded, Greenwood himself must surely have pondered upon the wisdom – or otherwise – of his decision not to go; because after having taken the lead in Norway, England fell apart as their opponents scored twice before half-time. Once again, the criticism became strident as the players and their manager were taken to task. It was Norway's first-ever victory over England, and they made the most of it … just as they made the most of their success against Graham Taylor's team in the run-up to the 1994 World Cup finals.

It was muck or nettles now for Greenwood's team, because while Hungary had to play at Wembley and England topped their group, all their rivals had matches in hand. But deliverance was at hand, too; because the Swiss won in Rumania and lost in Hungary, drew with Rumania in Berne … and the sequence of results meant that at Wembley, England could afford a draw against Hungary.

Hungary themselves had made certain of qualification, so there would be no pressure on them at Wembley, and Greenwood was encouraged sufficiently to tell his players that they had been given 'a kiss of life'. In the event, the match was scarcely remarkable for drama – the Hungarians did not produce anything to remind people of the Magical Magyars of the mid-1950's, while one goal, from Paul Mariner, was enough to ensure an England victory, which meant they had done the double over their fellow-travellers to the World Cup finals in Spain. Of course, there were those who could not help adding a little reminder … that Switzerland, too, had been England's allies along the way.

However, it seemed that if one problem had been solved, there was always another ready to rear its head – this time, there was discussion as to whether the home countries should be prepared to participate in a tournament which included Argentina – who had invaded the Falkland Islands and thus started a war with Britain. There was a threat from FIFA that the home countries risked being fined, should they pull out, but the actual outcome was settled as England won the war and it was decided that Ron Greenwood and his men could win football matches in Spain, as well. England were in a group which also consisted of Czechoslovakia, France and Kuwait (another nation which was to figure in a war that involved Britain, during the 1990's).

By the time England arrived in Bilbao, they had strung together a run of seven matches without defeat, and they tackled France 24 hours after the Falklands war had ended. It took them fewer than 30 seconds to score – Bryan Robson's effort was the fastest World Cup-final goal ever – and while France equalised, Robson struck again and Mariner made it 3-1. The next match was against the Czechs, and goals from Mariner and Francis did the trick, while Francis was on the mark once more in the 1-0 victory over Kuwait. That match was the major disappointment, since much more had been expected of England against a side of supposed no-hopers. Still, England could claim that they had achieved as much as Brazil, because they had been the only other nation to claim victory in all three of their games. Now England were switching from Bilbao to Madrid, where the opposition would come from the host country, and from their old adversaries, West Germany.

The Germans, of course, had arrived as European champions, and memories of previous, exciting encounters with England were revived. However, on the day the Germans played it tight, and there wasn't a goal in sight. Now everything hinged upon the outcome of Spain's games against England and the Germans, and the latter scored a 2-1 win against the host nation. The way the FIFA rules worked, it meant that if England and West Germany finished up level pegging, the issue would be decided by a draw – a decision which brought from the chairman of the Football Association, Professor Sir Harold Thompson, the comment that this was 'a bad day for the World Cup'. Bad day or not, it meant that in the final analysis, England would have to master the Spaniards 2-0 or 3-2 – a task not impossible, considering that they were out of contention, for starters, and that they had already been beaten by Northern Ireland, who were not considered to be the strongest opponents in the world.

Spain had one thing going for them, though; they would be playing in Real Madrid's famous Bernabeu stadium in front of a 75,000 crowd, most of whom would be rooting for the host country. And the atmosphere and support appeared to have stiffened the resolve of England's opponents, who held firm even if they were unable to score themselves. It was still 0-0 and the game was inside the final half-hour when England at last got their chances to deliver the much-needed scoreline. When Robson crossed the ball, Keegan was there, waiting to meet it, with the goal gaping before him. He rose and connected ... and sent his header wide. Brooking, too, had a scoring opportunity, but when he directed his effort on target, Spain's goalkeeper, Arconada, proved himself to be a worthy captain as he produced a tremendous save. So England's changes had been and gone, and the scoreless result meant that they were out, even as they remained undefeated after their five matches – five matches, come to that, in which they had conceded just a single goal. Now, at last, it was time for Greenwood to go; and he was able to retire with dignity and honour. He had done the job after Don Revie's defection, and he had rightly earned a vote of genuine appreciation from his bosses. More than this, he had given them time to sort out where they would go for his successor. And Bobby Robson emerged as the unanimous choice.

CHAPTER 9

AS Bruce Rioch began his first week in charge of team affairs at Arsenal, Bobby Robson was 1,000 miles away, in Portugal, where he was the manager of FC Porto. And Robson was talking about the might-have-beens as he reflected upon the chance of managing Arsenal… 'I wanted to go, but in the end, I would have had to walk out on Porto, and I was simply not prepared to do that'. Why not? – Plenty of other managers had turned their backs on clubs to go where they thought the grass would be greener. Loyalty was a subject on which Terry Venables, who had followed in Robson's footsteps as England team boss, expounded as he busied himself preparing his international players for Euro '96.

He was talking about the Inter Milan job which had just gone to another Englishman, Roy Hodgson (who had steered Switzerland to success), and El Tel revealed that while on holiday in Spain he had been approached by a representative who asked him: 'For any money, would you be able to leave now?' This representative was reported to have been acting on behalf of Inter's president, Massimo Moratti, though the Italian club did deny having offered the manager's job to Venables. In any event, Venables gave this answer: 'I happen to believe in loyalty and honouring contracts. The FA showed a lot of faith and courage when they appointed me. There was never any chance I would break my contract to take the Inter job'. His contract with England was due to expire after the European championships in the summer of 1996. Oddly enough, it had been Bobby Robson who, having put loyalty to Ipswich before an offer from Barcelona, recommended Venables to the Spanish club.

Barcelona took Venables (and enjoyed success with him in charge), Robson was persuaded to take on the England job (and he went close to a World Cup final) and by 1996 both men were talking about the maybes in their footballing lives. It seemed that before Rioch landed at Highbury, Arsenal had been prepared to offer Robson £400,000 a year if he would agree to become the director of football – and he admitted: 'There was a tremendous appeal in the prospect of returning to England and winning the title with them. I was flattered by their offer, which was for a very long term. But at the same time I believe I owe some loyalty to the Porto president'. Jorge Pinto da Costa had told Robson: 'This is your club; this is your home; this is where you must think about dying'. Robson reflected: 'I could not let him down – once before, I was faced with the decision of whether or not to walk out on a club. That was during my 13 years at Ipswich, when Barcelona wanted me. But I couldn't walk out on John Cobbold, who was chairman at that time, and I can't walk out on Jorge Pinto da Costa, either'.

There was more than a touch of irony about the Porto president's reference to dying, because Robson was to reached a stage shortly afterwards where he began to fear that he wouldn't even be alive to see the 1996 European championships. A cancer consultant reckoned that Robson would be dead inside nine months, unless he underwent emergency surgery. It had seemed to be no more than a routine check on a sinus problem from which Robson had suffered for more than 20 years, and, as he said after the consultant had delivered his verdict: 'I could not believe what the doctor was saying to me ... I said, look at me. I'm so fit and healthy. This cannot be true. No pain, no symptoms, no visible signs of ill-health. In fact, I had been annoyed with my wife for making the appointment. I simply didn't have the time to go. But every day now I thank God for her stubbornness... Elsie saved my life. In all probability I would not be here today if she hadn't insisted on me keeping that appointment'. I know exactly what he meant, because I had a similar traumatic experience – in my case, the doctor diagnosed angina and sent me to a specialist, asking me: 'You're not superstitious, are you?' – He had made the appointment for Friday the 13th.

The specialist told me I had a badly-blocked artery and so, like former Liverpool manager Graeme Souness, I underwent open-heart surgery. It was an emergency job, too – the law of averages said that with my problem I should really just have dropped dead. In Bobby Robson's case, his appointment in the summer of 1995 led to his undergoing surgery within 24 hours and, as the former England manager lay unconscious in the operating theatre, the surgeon deftly removed a large – and malignant – tumour which had been keeping itself hidden behind the cheekbone on the left side of Robson's face. While the operation was played down at the time, the 62-year-old Robson required 28 stitches after the tumour had been removed; then it was a matter of time doing the rest of the job with its healing process. And, of course, Robson was able, after all, to look forward to seeing England play in the European championships – by which time he had moved from Portugal to Spain.

Like Graham Taylor and others before him, he suffered during his spell as England manager, but he went on to steer PSV Eindhoven to the Dutch League title twice, and his next club, FC Porto, won the Cup and League in Portugal ... remarkably, one of the most successful runs in Robson's long and distinguished career was summarily ended towards the last days of March, 1996, when Porto – still 17 points clear at the top of the table – lost 2-1 to second-placed Benfica. That defeat ended an astonishing of 53 League games without defeat. Robson had also taken Porto to the semi-finals of the European Cup, and as he recovered from surgery it was made clear to him that his job was never in jeopardy. When he returned to work the Portuguese fans offered him a standing ovation, and he repaid them by ensuring his team retained the championship, as they won their League with three weeks to spare.

It was a sad day for Porto, and a wrench for Robson, when the parting of the ways came in May, 1996 – but when he left, he did so with the blessing of president Jorge Pinto da Costa. A phone call had started the ball rolling again, and it left Robson

Bobby Robson, who came so close to taking England to the World Cup Final in 1990.

saying: 'Nine months ago, I was told I could be dead by the end of the season ... instead, I have just been appointed manager of the biggest club in world football. Isn't life wonderful?' The club was Barcelona – who, at the third time of asking, had finally got their man.

Eight days previously, Robson had flown to London for a check-up, and been assured that his life-saving operation could be regarded as a success. Now, on the eve of the European championships, he was being offered a two-year contract by Barcelona worth, it was said, £2 million. He recalled how he had rejected the Spanish club twice ... 'but I knew I couldn't turn it down a third time, even though it was going to be an incredible wrench to leave FC Porto.' Having turned down Arsenal, after a personal plea from Jorge Pinto da Costa, Robson felt impelled to turn to his president and tell him that this time, he really did not believe he could say 'No'. Robson: 'I explained that at my time of life I would never get such an opportunity again. He understood. He's been a magnificent employer, and it has been a pleasure to work for him and the club.'

Not that it promised to be all smooth sailing, because Barcelona's sacking of Johan Cruyff brought down the wrath of the fans upon the head of the club, as the team played Celta Viga in the famous Nou Camp stadium. More than 50 supporters had to be restrained by security guards as they tried to attack the club's vice-president, and during the match dozens of fans held up banners carrying slogans against the Barcelona hierarchy and in favour of Cruyff, who had lost his job after eight years – most of them successful. The majority of the 70,000 crowd whistled and waved white handkerchiefs – the traditional Spanish protest – as club president José Luis Nunez arrived in the stadium. And all of this, of course, promised to make the arrival of Bobby Robson interesting, to say the least. His past record was impressive … but Barcelona demanded success in quick time…

I have long had a soft spot for the former England manager, and it all dates back to the now-distant days when he was the team boss at Ipswich. He did me what I considered to be a real favour – at a time when, I suppose, I could be numbered among the media pack. His team was due to play Manchester United at Old Trafford, and the evening before the game a national newspaper rang to ask me to contact Robson, who was staying with his team at a hotel about a dozen miles south of Manchester.

In the manner peculiar to newspapers, the matter was urgent – the *Daily Mail* had just learned that on the morrow Robson would be pitching an unknown, 17-year-old full-back into the fray at Old Trafford … and his direct opponent would be George Best. The message to me: 'Get hold of Robson, and ask if he'll let George Burley talk to you'. So I rang the Swan at Bucklow Hill and learned that the Ipswich manager was at dinner. He was good enough to interrupt his meal, come to the phone and answer my question by telling me: 'Yes, you can come down and talk to the lad – but give him time to finish his meal'. Inside half an hour I was sitting with young Burley and his room-mate, Kevin Beattie, and getting the kind of quotes the *Mail* required. Burley played, acquitted himself well, went on to play for Scotland and become a first-team regular at Ipswich … and by the spring of 1996 he was back at Portman Road, as the manager, and striving to take Town into the Premiership.

I always felt grateful to Bobby Robson for his courtesy and consideration – not least, because I knew that many other managers would have refused (and not too politely, either) on the grounds that they didn't want anything to distract a 17-year-old from going about his football business. I found Robson easy to talk to, as well, when his Ipswich team went to Anfield for a crunch match with Liverpool in the battle for the championship, and I did a piece with him for the match-day programme. It was, of course, Bill Shankly who famously declared that football was something which was of far greater significance than life or death … Bobby Robson, like me, now knows and admits that this is not the case at all. He came through surgery and, having considered everything, delivered this verdict: 'Football has been my life; it has been everything to me. But I can't say that any more, after what I have been through'. Like me, he recognised that when you have come face to face with the prospect of imminent death, you tend to get other things in true perspective. Football included. Even so, Robson – ever mindful of his own experiences in the job – remains a devout supporter of England. Indeed, he declared: 'I will never be critical of an England coach or manager. I had enough of that during my eight years in the job, and I vowed I would never do it myself'. There must be a moral in that, somewhere.

It might not be strictly true to say that Bobby Robson dragged himself up by his bootlaces, but he certainly had to work hard for what he achieved. Born on February 18, 1933, at Sacriston, County Durham, he was the son of a miner and one of five brothers. Football became a passion with him during his schoolboy days, as he played the game in the streets behind the terraced houses in Langley Park, a small mining village. As he grew up, the game became a way of life and, until he had reached his early 60's, he could claim to have been blessed with the good health so necessary for a career in which, as a player and as a manager, he had to suffer the slings and arrows of what Shakespeare called outrageous fortune. Robson's dad missed only one shift during 50 years down the pit, and Bobby could claim to have been similarly employed when it came to Soccer.

He did enjoy a round of golf – but scarcely had the time to get down to a golf course; he enjoyed going to the theatre – but evenings out were few and far between, because too often he was busy watching a match. There was little or no time for reading – except when he was travelling on a long coach journey or taking to the air with his team. He married a former nurse who became a primary-school teacher, and his three sons all were sent to public schools – like their, mother, they saw less of him than most families see of the bread-winner. But if the Robson boys went to public schools, their father worked hard for them – in fact, during his playing days he did some coaching on the side ... admitting later that this was in order to make money to live. As a player, he had a distinguished career; as a manager, he soon knew what it was to be given the sack ... and if it scarred him, it also taught him something. Along the way, he also because the longest-serving manager in the country, as he enjoyed an unbroken spell at Ipswich Town from 1969 until he took the England job in the summer of 1982.

Robson's first professional club was Fulham – he signed for the Craven Cottage club in 1950 and made 152 first-team appearances, scoring 68 goals. By 1956 he was playing for West Brom, and with them he totalled 239 games and scored 56 goals. From 1962 to 1967 it was back to Craven Cottage, and 193 more games for Fulham (plus nine goals). By that time, he had graduated as an England player, with 20 appearances to his credit and a tally of four goals. And then he broke into management.

He suffered two unhappy – and worrying – experiences, because he went to Canada to take charge of a team called Vancouver Royals … and discovered, too late, that he had made a big mistake. The same thing happened at Fulham. It was while his playing days there were drawing to a close that he received an offer to go to Vancouver, a beautiful city, as I can confirm from first-hand knowledge. Robson had been there with West Brom and had been impressed, too. What was more, the Royals were ready to pay him £7,000 a year – double his pay at Fulham – and so he sailed off in the Oriana to rediscover Vancouver and build a new career. It went horribly wrong. because the club franchise was taken over by someone who decided that the former Hungarian star, Ferenc Puskas, should be given a coaching job. For Robson, that made life difficult, not least because of the language problem … and he had already found that there were problems when it came to being paid.

Months went by, and Robson began a battle to gain compensation through the courts; however, before things could be finalised, he was contacted by Fulham and asked to return as their manager. He took a salary cut of almost 50 percent – and learned, as the Royals went bust, that he could have been waiting till kingdom come for his money. At that stage of the game, Fulham looked like a heaven-sent escape route. But no more than nine months later Robson tasted what it was like to be sacked. And, as has happened to other team bosses, he learned his fate from the papers. Robson then was left to reflect upon the way his career in football had gone, so far. He had started out as a player by going to Ayresome Park and having trials with Middlesbrough, then he spent a month at Southampton. Boro' said nothing, the Saints said good-bye – then, when he had reached the age of 17 (when a club could actually sign a youngster), Middlesbrough, Southampton, Newcastle United, Huddersfield Town, York City, Blackpool, Lincoln City and Fulham all beat a path to his door.

Robson had been put off by his earlier experiences at Ayresome and The Dell; Newcastle, although his favourites, had a reputation for signing big-name players, rather than grooming local talent; and as for Fulham, it was their manager. Bill Dodgin (whose name was synonymous with the club) who was the most persuasive.

The pay was £7 a week, but there were one or two strings attached … such as the fact that Robson's father insisted he should keep up his apprenticeship as an electrical engineer and carry on going to night school. However, it was at Craven Cottage that Robson learned his trade, in company with other players such as Johnny Haynes, Jimmy Hill, Charlie Mitten, Bedford Jezzard and Tony Macedo. Even in those days, Jimmy Hill had innovative ideas on the coaching side of the game – it was Hill who, when manager of Coventry City, answered his critics who accused him of being a 'gimmick' man as he told me: 'A gimmick is something other people wish they'd thought of first'. He could have been right, at that.

Fulham in those days had the comedian, Tommy Trinder, as their chairman, And there were quite a few people who thought Trinder was more than a comedian when he agreed to make Haynes English football's first £100-a-week footballer. By the time Bobby Robson had returned from Vancouver and stepped into the manager's job at Craven Cottage, Trinder's role as chairman was being usurped by a man called Sir Eric Miller. So far as Robson was concerned, it was not a happy association. In the time that it takes to start and produce a family – nine months – Robson was in and out – sacked by Miller, and describing it as 'a shattering experience'. According to Robson, Miller wanted to have a finger in almost every pie – team selection, buying and selling of players – and when the manager fought back, he was given the order of the boot, with Haynes being named as his replacement. Robson had no grudge against Haynes, but he didn't take kindly to Sir Eric Miller, and after the financier had committed suicide by shooting himself, Robson was prompted to observe: 'Shows how he stood up to pressure, didn't it?' Robson thus became the 686th managerial casualty since the second world war had ended … and he learned what it was like to stand in the dole queue, as he spent three months out of work during the winter of season 1968-69.

He was offered some part-time scouting by Dave Sexton and was despatched to check on a match between Ipswich and Nottingham Forest – both clubs were without managers. So he applied for the job at Ipswich, although two other big names, Billy Bingham and Frank O'Farrell, were rated the front runners. The former stayed with Plymouth Argyle, O'Farrell remained at Torquay … and Robson got the job, on a verbal promise that he would be given at least two years.

He was to express the view later than a manager needed three years, in order to impose his own style on a club; as it turned out, Robson stayed at Ipswich for 13 years, during which time they carried off the FA Cup (in 1978) and the UEFA Cup (in 1981). In seasons 1980-81 and 1981-82 Ipswich Town finished as First Division runners-up, and it was a matter of lasting regret to Bobby Robson that he never quite made it to the pinnacle, as it were, in English football – although he remedied this by steering both PSV Eindhoven and FC Porto to their respective championships. Robson's reign at Portman Road lasted from January, 1969, until July, 1982, when he was handed the task of overseeing England's progress hopefully through to the finals of the World Cup. He was to say later that his time at Ipswich was the happiest of his life … he turned down the chance to manage Barcelona, Bilbao, Aston Villa, Derby County, Everton, Leeds United, Manchester United, Newcastle United, Sunderland and Wolves, at various times and it was only when he was asked to take on what he considered to be the top job of all – managing England – that he felt he had been made an offer he couldn't refuse.

It wasn't always a bed of roses at Portman Road – Robson had battles with players (and their wives!) and fell foul of the fans … he actually heard them chanting 'Robson out! Robson out!' in much the same way that, in the spring of 1996, Howard Wilkinson heard the taunts of the Leeds fans as his team was beaten by Aston Villa in the final of the Coca-Cola Cup at Wembley. As Wilkinson said then: 'It hurts'. Robson always gave heartfelt credit to the Cobbolds at Ipswich for their tolerance and their kindness and after he had suffered from the jeers of the crowd he attended a board meeting at which the chairman, John Cobbold, made it the first item on the agenda to apologize for the bad behaviour of the fans the previous evening. And when Ipswich languished at the foot of the table, Robson was offered a new contract... The directors' gesture of faith in their manager was amply rewarded, as the years rolled by. The FA Cup, the UEFA Cup, almost the League championship – plus money in the bank, a team which played with some flair, and a ground which underwent considerable improvement. All these things came to pass during Robson's time at Portman Road. Even so, he was to experience more than a few problems; when it was Wembley time in the FA Cup, for instance.

What has been termed 'people power' – a backlash from the fans – has led to more than one manager being shown the exit door. In Robson's case, as the FA Cup final loomed in 1978, it was his first (and last) experience of 'player power' which became imprinted upon his memory. For once, his Ipswich footballers decided to make their feelings known as they objected to the team Robson proposed to put out. When Ipswich played at Villa Park, immediately before the final against Arsenal, Robson recalled Colin Viljoen (fit again after having been out since February), switched Brian Talbot to right-half as the replacement for Roger Osborne and John Wark to Talbot's usual left-half spot. Talbot made it clear he wasn't happy about this and, according to Robson, Viljoen was not exactly the flavour of the month with team-mates.

Aston Villa hammered Ipswich 6-1 and, again according to Robson, it was clear to him that some of his players had been giving less than 100 percent In his own words, 'they didn't respond to Viljoen, and some were loath to give him the ball'. Robson admitted that he hadn't appreciated the depth of resentment there was, but – not surprisingly – he was furious about the Villa Park display, in which stand-in 'keeper Paul Overton (an 18-year-old apprentice) had turned out to be the team's best player. 'But for him,' Robson lashed his other players, 'we would have lost by 10 goals. That says a lot about you...' At the same time, of course, the manager knew full well, and so did the players, that he could not dump them for the Wembley date.

He reverted to the midfield of Talbot, Wark and Osborne, told Viljoen it had been a mistake to recall him, and the player – while accepting this verdict – claimed (rightly, in Robson's view) that he had been the victim of 'player power'. So Viljoen stayed home while Ipswich went to their pre-Wembley headquarters, while at the same time giving his side of the story to a reporter. It was the biggest week in Ipswich Town's history, it meant unwelcome publicity – but, said Robson, it had cleared the air. The 'player-power' war was over; all that was left was for the team to prove the knockers wrong ... because Arsenal were rated racing certs. to walk off with the FA Cup. The pressure was off Ipswich to such an extent that their players were relaxed right through the days up to the final, and they went to Wembley with the intention of enjoying their big day out.

That they did, and to some tune. It may not have been the greatest final in the history of the FA Cup, but it certainly belonged to under-dogs Ipswich. David Geddis, a 20-year-old reserve signed from Carlisle United, had been pitched in alongside striker Paul Mariner, and it was Geddis – playing 'possibly the finest game of his career', according to his manager – who put Sammy Nelson in his pocket while contriving to add something to the Ipswich style. When Geddis crossed the ball, centre-half Willie Young – the Scot who was built like the trunk of an oak tree – could do no better than mishit it, and Osborne snapped up the opportunity to beat Pat Jennings. There were just under 15 minutes to go ... and with that match-winner, Osborne had done. As trainer Cyril Lea told Robson: 'His legs have gone ... he'll have to come off'. And he did. But Ipswich hung on to claim the Cup – and Osborne became a member of the Robson family, in a sense, because the manager named his dog Roger.

Season 1980-81 promised to top that FA Cup triumph, because Ipswich were going for a treble: League title, FA Cup and UEFA Cup. They finished second in the League, faltered also in the FA Cup, but landed the European trophy. No fewer than seven first-teamers suffered injuries at various times, and Ipswich were not a club which could carry a massive playing staff. Yet they carried on through 66 matches – and when they met FC Cologne in the UEFA Cup, the German officials, staggered by Town's work load, told Robson: 'You English are crazy ... it's impossible to play so many matches'. Ipswich had won their first League game (1-0 at Leicester), beaten Brighton and drawn at Stoke, then shot to the top of the table with a 4-0 hammering of Everton. They beat Aston Villa and Crystal Palace, then got through their first UEFA Cup match comfortably, beating Aris Salonika 5-1 at Portman Road.

Coventry City went down 2-0, and by the end of September, after having met Wolves, Ipswich still topped the table. However, the Greeks won the UEFA Cup return 3-0, so Ipswich just squeezed through; then a home draw (1-1) against Leeds United was followed by Town's second victory in the League Cup (Middlesbrough first, then East Anglian rivals Norwich City). One big test was at Anfield, where Ipswich drew 1-1 with Liverpool, and the result was similar against Manchester United at Portman Road. In the UEFA Cup against Bohemians, of Prague, a 3-0 victory in the home leg ensured a 3-2 aggregate success.

Meanwhile, Sunderland fell at Roker Park, but Birmingham won the League Cup-tie on their own ground and a home point was dropped against West Brom. Ipswich shared half a dozen goals at Southampton, then lost their first League match (1-0 at Brighton), by which time it was almost mid-November. There followed victories over Leicester City and Nottingham Forest in the League, and a 5-0 hiding for Widzew Lodz in the UEFA Cup duel at Portman Road. By early December, after a draw at

Maine Road, Ipswich had slipped to third in the table, but they came through the UEFA Cup return, having lost by the only goal in Poland. So, on December 13, it was Liverpool at Portman Road, in front of 32,000 fans, and the result was 1-1 again.

A 5-3 defeat at White Hart Lane in mid-December was only the second League defeat for Ipswich, then they won 3-1 at Birmingham, beat Norwich 2-0 on home ground and drew 1-1 with Arsenal at Highbury. Aston Villa went out of the FA Cup at Portman Road, Ipswich completed a League double over Nottingham Forest and drilled five goals past Birmingham to go top again – a position they held with a 0-0 draw at Goodison Park. In the FA Cup, it was 0-0 at Shrewsbury, 3-0 in the return, while Stoke went down 4-0, Crystal Palace lost 3-2, and Charlton were knocked out of the FA Cup in round five. Next came a 1-0 win over Middlesbrough and a 3-1 success against Wolves, followed by a 4-0 triumph against Coventry City ... and a brilliant demolition job away on St. Etienne, who forged ahead – then lost 4-1.

In the FA Cup, Nottingham Forest shared six goals with Ipswich but lost the replay, then Ipswich beat Spurs 3-0 and carried on by slamming St. Etienne 7-2 overall in the UEFA Cup. However, there followed a 2-1 defeat at Old Trafford – then a 4-1 home win over Sunderland, to round off the month. Well, almost ... because on the last day of March, Ipswich went to Leeds and suffered their heaviest defeat (3-0) of the season. They were starting a spell of 10 games in 33 days, and at The Hawthorns West Brom won 3-1. By then, Ipswich had been knocked off the top of the table by Aston Villa, and they faced FC Cologne in the first leg of their UEFA Cup semi-final. At Portman Road it was 1-0 for Robson's men, and in the semi-final of the FA Cup, against Manchester City at Villa Park, there was a similar scoreline ... in City's favour. One down, two to go.

It was then mid-April, and Ipswich were coming up to their 58th game of the season – away, at Villa Park. Few people gave Ipswich a chance, but they staggered the critics by winning 2-1 ... then, four days later, Arsenal won 2-0 at Portman Road. The good work had been undone. It was Norwich City away, minus five senior players, and the Canaries were chirping over a 1-0 victory, which took Ipswich into the UEFA Cup return against Cologne. A second-half goal from Terry Butcher saw Ipswich through, 2-0 on aggregate, but after beating Manchester City 1-0 and leading 1-0 at Ayresome Park, they lost to Middlesbrough ... and so did Aston Villa, at Highbury. It was the beginning of May, and the 64th game was looming – against AZ'67 Alkmaar in the Portman Road leg of the UEFA Cup final.

Alkmaar had just beaten Feyenoord 5-1 (they were to give Liverpool a fright on another European night), but at Portman Road Ipswich gained the upper hand with a 3-0 win. However, before the return, they had to tackle Southampton and, with Aston Villa by then assured of the League title, maybe Ipswich minds were on the UEFA Cup – certainly Southampton were up for it, because they were out to qualify for Europe. The Saints won, 3-2, and Robson warned his players that they must do better in the second leg of the European contest. As expected, Alkmaar went for goals, and they got them ... four of them. But with Ipswich also in scoring mood, the outcome was an aggregate, 5-4 triumph which took the trophy to Portman Road.

CHAPTER 10

BOBBY ROBSON accepted a job as manager of Everton – then gave the Goodison club backword, after the story had leaked out to the newspapers before he had had the chance to tell his chairman at Ipswich. He also had the offer of the Manchester United job from chairman Martin Edwards (in May, 1981), and turned that down – at the time, he was more interested in going back to his native North-East, where he was wanted by Sunderland … and before all this, he had rejected overtures from Derby County and Leeds United, who asked him to follow Don Revie, the then new England manager. Newcastle United also had a go at trying to persuade Robson to make the switch from Ipswich, and from Spain there were approaches by Barcelona and Bilbao. In some instances, the money on offer amounted to a fortune, but for one reason or another Robson remained the manager of Ipswich Town.

In the summer of 1981, Sunderland offered to double the salary he was getting at Portman Road and make him the best-paid manager in Britain – with a contract for as long as Robson wanted. True, it wasn't the £80,000 a year (plus £35,000 guaranteed bonuses) which Barcelona had offered, but Robson had a soft spot for Sunderland. In the end, however, he remained at Ipswich – probably, as he said later, because of the club's UEFA Cup triumph. Robson, being Robson, told his chairman about the Sunderland offer, and was told he could have a 10-year contract at Ipswich … the only way he would be allowed to leave, with the club's blessing, was if he were offered, and wished to accept, the job of managing England. So that was how, after 13 eventful years at Portman Road, Bobby Robson finally came to bow out.

When he was appointed manager of the national team, in July, 1982, he left Ipswich knowing that the club had been built on solid foundations; when he left the England job in July, 1990, he knew that he had gone tantalisingly close to emulating his predecessor at Portman Road, Sir Alf Ramsey. And in between times, he had ridden a roller-coaster as England's fortunes had ebbed and flowed. His first match in charge was a European-championship qualifying match against Denmark in Copenhagen. The result: 2-2. His next date was one of destiny … England versus West Germany, at Wembley. The result: 1-2. Not until the third game – another European-championship qualifier, against Greece in Salonika, could Robson claim a victory (3-0) … and then came a deluge of goals, as England thrashed hapless Luxembourg 9-0 at Wembley to win another qualifying match.

Wembley wasn't all glory, despite that Luther Blissett hat-trick in the demolition job on Luxembourg … it took the odd goal in three to beat Wales there, while Greece came, saw – and held out for a scoreless draw in their qualifier for the European championships. Hungary were then beaten 2-0 at Wembley, as were the old enemy,

Scotland (though Northern Ireland held England to a 0-0 draw in Belfast). After Scotland, it was a trip down under, and in Australia there were two draws and a 1-0 win against the Aussie national side. By then, it was June, 1983, and shortly there would be more European qualifiers – against Denmark at Wembley, and away against Hungary and Luxembourg. There were tears, not cheers, after the Danes had scored the only goal; but England rallied to win 3-0 and 4-0 on their travels abroad. By the time June, 1984, had come round, Robson's England had played eight more matches, with varying results ... defeats by France (in Paris), Wales (at Wrexham), Russia (at Wembley) and Uruguay (in Montevideo); draws against Scotland (at Hampden) and Chile (in Santiago); victory over Northern Ireland at Wembley ... and a glorious triumph against Brazil in Rio de Janeiro, where John Barnes struck a memorable, spectacular goal in the 2-0 win.

Season 1984-85 marked the start of the really big games; the World Cup qualifying matches against Finland, Turkey, Northern Ireland and Rumania. Robson himself was to confess that his first couple of years in the international hot seat were difficult indeed, notably when it came to the European championships.

When it came to Europe, there could be only one qualifier from each of the eight groups, so this meant there could be no mistakes – as Robson discovered when the Wembley defeat by Denmark cost England their chance of a place in the finals. It was to be the sole defeat in a qualifier during his eight-year reign as the national team boss; but it was still no consolation at the time. When it came to the World Cup, on paper it seemed things might be somewhat easier, in terms of qualifying but, of course, the critics were always ready to start sniping at the first opportunity ... and they had been given ammunition right at the outset of Robson's international haul when he axed Kevin Keegan. When Robson attended a match at Newcastle, where Keegan was an idol as he drove the Magpies on towards promotion, the England manager was spat upon and verbally abused. It was, he declared 'a little taste' of what he had to put up with during the rest of his stewardship. And, of course, when Denmark did the business against England at Wembley in September, 1983, that became just about the blackest day to date in Robson's whole career,

By the time England travelled to Brazil, Robson was a target for the media and Barcelona were on his trail again, presumably basing their bid to lure him on the fact that the international job was proving such a headache. However, as before, Robson said 'Thanks, but no, thanks' – he intended to see out the three remaining years of his England contract; and that was when he recommended Terry Venables for the job in Spain. His own career received a timely injection of good cheer with that win in Brazil, and there was reason for optimism with the grouping of Finland, Northern Ireland, Turkey and Rumania in the battle for a World Cup spot in Mexico. Down went the Finns as England scored a nap hand of goals at Wembley; down went the Turks as England rattled in eight goals in Istanbul. And then England went to

Belfast and beat Northern Ireland by the only goal of the game. Now they were on their way ... they had won in Brazil for the first time, they had scored 14 goals without conceding one, in their three World Cup qualifiers, and when they drew against Finland in the return and against Rumania away, the final three outings looked to be a formality. Rumania at Wembley, Turkey at Wembley, and Northern Ireland at Wembley.

However, there followed defeat by Scotland at Hampden – accompanied by a demand from one tabloid daily that Robson should go. He didn't of course – although he and his players did go to Mexico City to acclimatise, in preparation for the forthcoming World Cup ... always assuming England still managed to qualify. This they did, with draws against Rumania and Northern Ireland, while the Turks were hammered 5-0. So it was definitely Mexico, here we come; but before all this, England's pre-World Cup trip to Mexico and the United States in the summer of '85 coincided with news of the Heysel-stadium disaster and, for a while, there were fears that as English clubs became exiled from European competition, the England international team might find itself excluded from the World Cup. This didn't happen, so England, having finished at the head of their qualifying group, learned that in the World Cup proper they would have to take on Portugal, Morocco and Poland.

Warm-up matches gave England a feeling of some security, as they reeled off an unbeaten run which stretched through no fewer than 11 games; but when it came to the real thing, Portugal scored the only goal in the opener in Monterrey and the so-called no-hopers from Morocco made light of the 100-degree temperature while England sweated and strained to stay level with them. That match finished 0-0, then it was on to the duel with Poland, who had beaten the Portuguese. The match became a personal triumph for Gary Lineker as he struck three goals, and so it was on from Monterrey to Mexico City and a date with Paraguay.

It was Lineker who struck once more; then he went off injured, and Peter Beardsley made it 2-0 ... which was the signal for Lineker to return and hit a third goal. In the Aztec stadium four days later, England tried conclusions with Argentina, and Maradona scored a goal with his fist. Peter Shilton, who had gone up to challenge Maradona, protested furiously, but the 'hand of God' goal was allowed to stand, and the chunky little Argentinian did more damage when he wove his way through the England defence and scored again. This time no-one could doubt the quality of his goal. Even then, England were not finished ... Lineker scored, but England were running out of time ... and out of the World Cup ... while Argentina went on to the final and wound up as winners of the coveted trophy.

Season 1986-87 brought the European-championship qualifying matches again, and the draw pitched England in with Northern Ireland, Turkey and Yugoslavia, so there was a familiar ring about all this. By the time the next World Cup qualifiers came round, England would have played 21 more games and remained unbeaten in

16 of them, with nine victories to their credit – including one 8-0 result and two more matches in which they scored four goals each time ... after having kicked off by losing 1-0 against Sweden in Stockholm. But they started the qualifying matches with a 3-0 success against Northern Ireland at Wembley, where Lineker again confirmed his ability as a marksman, with two of the goals, then they scored a 2-0 win over Yugoslavia at the same venue. Full points, so far, on the way to the European championships.

Morale was boosted even higher with a 4-2 victory over Spain in Madrid – all four goals came from Lineker, who by this time had left Everton and was playing for Terry Venables and Barcelona. The trip to Belfast for the return against Northern Ireland brought a 2-0 victory, but there was some disappointment when England were held to a scoreless draw by Turkey in Izmir, not least because of the way they had rattled in goals against the Turks in previous encounters, There were draws against Brazil (at Wembley) and Scotland (in Glasgow), and then came a 3-1 defeat by West Germany in Dusseldorf, five weeks before the Wembley return against the Turks. That defeat, however, was to be forgotten as England ran riot at Wembley ... a hat-trick from Lineker, two goals from Barnes, with Beardsley, Webb and Robson each chipping in. And the following month, in November, 1987, Yugoslavia were given a tousing on their own turf – 4-1 ... and this without even one goal from Lineker, who in 17 outings with England scored no fewer than 20 goals.

There were half a dozen matches before the European championships proper, and England's travels took them to Tel Aviv, Budapest and Lausanne, as well as to Wembley for three games there. Draws against Israel, Holland and Hungary were followed by victories over Scotland and the Swiss, with another draw (against Colombia) sandwiched in between those two results. And then it was into Europe for the chance of taking the big prize.

By this time, for a change, Robson and his players were being given plenty of praise for their efforts – and deservedly so. But it doesn't take long for the bouquets to turn to brickbats – and it was an Englishman, Jack Charlton, who had the job of planning England's downfall when they took on the Republic of Ireland in Stuttgart. With only five minutes gone Ray Houghton put the Irish ahead, so England had to set about the job of going for goals. They attacked in numbers, with Lineker cursing his luck, Hoddle seeing an effort beat 'keeper Pat Bonner but slip past a post, and Beardsley slipping up right in front of the target. After all this, Houghton's goal turned out to be the winner.

England travelled on from Stuttgart to Dusseldorf and then to Frankfurt; and disaster travelled with them. First, there was a 3-1 defeat at the hands of Holland, and next came a similar scoreline as Russia did the business. Dutch ace Marco van Basten scored a brilliant hat-trick, although England twice hit the woodwork. England then knew that they could book their flight home – but before that, they had to meet the Russians … and that match was a real downer for Robson. Against the Irish and the Dutch, England had at least shown skill and effort, and Robson believed they had played well enough to have deserved some reward … against Russia, his players did not do themselves justice. And that was putting it kindly. Robson himself admitted that his team's display made him ashamed. 'I had asked them to play for pride and give a performance for their country; but we capitulated'.

England's manager could have no doubts about one thing; the knives were out after this sorry ending to the bid for European glory. There was a Wembley date with Denmark before the first of the World Cup qualifiers came up, and it was imperative that England salvaged something of their reputation. They managed a single-goal victory over the Danes at Wembley (the goal came from Webb), and then it was into World Cup action against Sweden there. The match ended without either side having a goal to show for their efforts. That was a period which Robson confessed was one of the worst in his career – in fact, even before the World Cup qualifiers came along he had become the target for the 'Sack him' brigade.

He was fortunate that in Bert Millichip he had a genuine backer – just as the chairman of the Football Association backed Terry Venables *en route* to the 1996 European championships, so he gave Bobby Robson an assurance that his job was safe. He asked Robson if he could take the pressure, making it plain that the Football Association was ready to stand firm. And when Robson replied that he could, Millichip told him: 'Carry on, and get us to the World Cup finals'. So the summer of 1988 passed, and after the opening match of season 1988-89 had brought that lone-goal victory over Denmark and the 0-0 draw against the Swedes, Robson's England battled on. As Robson said, every match was 'dynamite'. And a 1-1 draw against Saudi Arabia in the Middle East did nothing to quell the demands for Robson's head. The old Army tag of 'Desert Rats' was changed to 'Desert Prats', and it was 'Go, for the love of Allah' as the headlines blasted England's team boss.

When he returned from Riyadh it was chaotic at Heathrow airport, where it seemed that every reporter in the land had gathered, with just one question to ask: 'When are you going to quit?' Meanwhile, the cameras clicked and the flashbulbs popped and, as Robson found himself being jostled by the throng, he needed the strong arms of the law to protect him. Don Howe, one of Robson's aides, was so indignant at the treatment Robson received that he told the England team boss … if it had been him, then he would have turned his back on the job. But the defiant chairman of the Football Association stood up and told the assembled media that there was NO question of Robson being sacked. And the manager could take some comfort, also, from the fact that as the media screamed for his head, the general public began to resent this to the extent that there was a backlash, with Robson gaining support from the fans.

The vultures were still hovering when England went to Athens in February, 1989, to tackle Greece in another friendly, and only a few minutes into the match Robson's team conceded a penalty. Fortunately for the players and their manager, they hit back with a couple of goals, to return home victorious. But there were two World Cup qualifiers on the horizon which spelled more danger ... Albania in Tirana, and then at Wembley. The second date should not be much of a worry, but the trip to Tirana posed several headaches.

I have yet to meet a manager or a player who will admit to looking forward to a trip to Albania – it's a country regarded as being virtually an unknown quantity to folk from western Europe. Robson's England, however, stood up manfully to the task in Tirana, and after 90 minutes they were enjoying the feeling of victory, with a 2-0 result in the bag. The Wembley date with Albania began to appear considerably more inviting, and five goals without reply said it all. Yet even then, there had been a pre-match problem. Once upon a time, not so long ago, England's participation in the World Cup had been put at risk by the Heysel disaster ... and just before the Wembley date with Albania there was the tragedy of Hillsborough. As the whole of the country mourned, Merseyside in particular was in a state of shock – Liverpool Football Club virtually closed down and, as I can confirm (since at the time I was working for Liverpool), it was a matter of treading so carefully, walking on eggshells in the effort not to cause further grief to anyone.

The Liverpool players were no longer appearing on a Saturday afternoon, and there was even a question as to whether or not they should pull out of the FA Cup, after the semi-final disaster at Hillsborough. The players and their wives were counselling the bereaved and John Barnes, for one, had made a commitment to one of the families which he felt he could not break – even when it came to playing for his country in a World Cup qualifier. So Barnes was missing from the side to take on Albania at Wembley, although by that time other Liverpool stars such as Beardsley and McMahon had decided they could face up to playing football again. Beardsley did line up against the Albanians – and he was a two-goal marksman in the 5-0 victory.

Chile at Wembley and Scotland at Hampden Park produced a 0-0 draw and a 2-0 win for England, respectively, and so the Poles were next on the agenda – this one another World Cup outing, with Wembley the venue. Barnes was back for England – and, along with Lineker and Webb, he was on the mark in a 3-0 victory. Then it was off to Copenhagen, for a 1-1 draw with the Danes, before a date with Sweden in Stockholm in September, 1989, for another World Cup qualifier. The time was flying by, and the World Cup finals were looming closer and closer.

By the time England played in Stockholm, the team's stock – and that of their manager – had risen, on the back of 10 matches without one defeat. If the failure in Europe had not exactly been forgotten or forgiven by the critics, at least now there was renewed hope for the World Cup in Italy in 1990 ... always provided that England didn't cock it up again, on the final run-in. The match in Sweden ended with Robson paying 'keeper Peter Shilton a massive tribute for the part he had played in ensuring the scoreless draw. England had had to do without Bryan Robson, while Terry Butcher – named captain in his place – became another hero in a white shirt which, during the heat of the action, also became stained with his blood. Butcher had suffered a bad head injury – it required 15 stitches – but he stayed on the field, his head swathed in a thick bandage that also showed signs of the blood he had shed. Overall, and considering the problems he had had to endure, Bobby Robson could consider this to have been a job well done. There now remained just one more qualifying match, and that was against Poland, in Katowice.

Mention of Poland brought back memories of a previous World Cup campaign under Robson's predecessor at Ipswich, Sir Alf Ramsey... Poland had been the country which effectively brought his international reign to a conclusion, as England failed to get the result they needed, and a goalkeeper who had been labelled by Brian Clough as 'a clown' had barred the route to goal with just about every part of his body. Now, in October, 1989, Katowice was the final calling place for Robson's team. Once again, Shilton turned out to be the hero of the hour, as the Poles – with a vastly altered side – drove forward in their bid to rattle in the goals. The greatest threat came right at the end of the game, when a 30-yard drive did beat the England 'keeper ... but he saw it shudder the bar. Shilton then was coming up to his 40th birthday, and he had defied the years as well as opposing forwards to such an extent that he had not conceded one goal during the World Cup qualifying matches. That was some record to take into the World Cup finals themselves. Robson now had some breathing space – from October, 1989, to June, 1990 when the World Cup finals kicked off ... but he knew he needed to use that breathing space to the greatest advantage.

CHAPTER 11

WEMBLEY was the venue for half a dozen of England's World Cup warm-up matches between October, 1989, and May, 1990. Then Bobby Robson and his players would take themselves off to Tunisia for one final game in preparation for the real thing in Italy. He looked ahead, and he came to a decision that what his team needed was some really useful opposition on which to flex their muscles. He came up with Italy at Wembley, for starters, then Yugoslavia, Brazil, Czechoslovakia and Denmark, and, to round it all off, Uruguay. Among that little lot was the country which would be hosting the 1990 World Cup finals, and former World Cup champions in Brazil, plus the country which had emerged as European champions, Denmark. The Yugoslavs, the Czechs and the Uruguayans could not be considered easy opposition, either. No fewer than five of the teams England were to face would be appearing on the World Cup stage in Italy, while the host nation, along with Brazil, were rated as favourites to win the tournament.

The first match ended in a scoreless draw, and the critics began to unload their ammunition once more ... they pointed out that England had failed to unlock the Italian defence, and that Italy had long had a reputation for being able to contain their opponents while breaking away to do damage themselves. Robson himself was satisfied with the performance; as for the result, he claimed that his team could easily have come away from Wembley with a 2-0 victory to their credit. But, at the end of the night, there did remain a problem ... England had to find a solution up front, after just one goal in four drawn games.

Cometh the hour, cometh the man – Bryan Robson, who made December 13 a lucky night for England as he scored against Yugoslavia after only 38 seconds – the fastest-ever goal scored at Wembley by an England player. Yugoslavia were not easy to beat, and they had arrived after having licked Scotland and topped their qualifying group, but they became England's 100th victims at the famous old stadium as Robson struck a second goal, to make the result 2-1. That made it 14 matches without defeat for Bobby Robson's team, and there were three more victories on the trot as England disposed of Brazil (1-0), the Czechs (4-2) and the Danes (1-0). The Brazilians had won in Holland and Italy, and they were looking like the team all the others would have to beat, to carry off the World Cup. Lineker was the match-winner. England had now played Brazil three times ... winning home and away and being unbeaten against them.

England signed off at Wembley with their game against Uruguay – and lost there for the first time in six years, although only by the odd goal in three. Then it was off to Tunis for the final warm-up and acclimatization before the start of the World Cup tournament in Cagliari, where Jack Charlton's Republic of Ireland would be waiting. Between Tunis and Cagliari, however, there was a week in Sardinia for the England squad – in fact, Robson's team travelled from Sardinia to Tunis for the final warm-up match, which ended 1-1 ... thanks to a last-minute face-saver from substitute Steve Bull. There were nine days to go before the World Cup kick-off against the Republic of Ireland, although the tournament actually had begun on Friday, June 8, with the match between holders Argentina and the outsiders from Cameroon.

That game produced an upset as Cameroon defeated Argentina, Diego Maradona and all – even after the African side had two players sent off. Cameroon kept a tight rein on Maradona, and they served notice that other teams who took them lightly would do so at their peril. The ruling body of football, FIFA, also had served notice ... that players and teams must toe the line when it came to discipline on the field of play; and the referees were under orders to go strictly by the book, so that any indiscretions – even the slightest – were likely to come in for punishment.

As the England players awaited their encounter with the Republic of Ireland, other matches were going on: Czechoslovakia destroyed the United States with a five-goal salvo, West Germany made everyone take notice as they struck four goals against Yugoslavia, and Brazil were impressive winners against Sweden, even if they had to rely upon the odd goal in three. So far as England were concerned, the Germans were the ones to miss, because they appeared to be the outstanding side – although, of course, time would tell. Time certainly told on Scotland ... over 90 minutes against unrated Costa Rica little went right, and the Scots were looking stunned as they walked off, a beaten team. In a few hours' time Bobby Robson would know whether or not his England side had triumphed – or gone the way of the Scots. One thing was for sure – there could be no excuses about players being missing; he was able to choose his team from a full-strength squad, and when he named the side it didn't differ much from the one which had lost to Jack Charlton's men in the European championships.

The pre-match planning had taken into account the weather, which was expected to be warm, almost balmy ... instead, there was a gale and lightening flashed as the clouds became black and heavy. England kicked off playing against the wind and inside 10 minutes they had scored, as Lineker finished off a move which involved Waddle, who curled the ball goalwards. The Irish reacted strongly and Shilton, in his 119th appearance for England (thus equalling a record) was kept busy; but it was still 1-0 at half-time, and then Robson's men would have the wind in their favour ... or would they? – Seemingly not, because as the players rested for the 15-minute interval, the storm arrived and, with it, the wind died down. The second half was nothing to write home about, either, though England's appeal for a penalty after Waddle had been downed fell upon deaf ears.

There were twenty minutes to go, and Jack Chalton was clearly becoming an anxious man, as he switched things around by replacing John Aldridge with Alan McLoughlin – so Robson countered by replacing Beardsley with his Liverpool team-mate, McMahon … who misplaced a pass intended for Waddle and saw it fall just right for Kevin Sheedy, ironically one of Everton's players at club level. He packed a deadly left-foot shot, and he drilled the ball past Shilton to save the Irish bacon. Jack Charlton was beaming, as he saw his side get away with the draw.

At the post-match inquest, Robson was required to defend his team's display, as the critics got to work; then he had to plan for the next match, against the Dutch. He saw them draw 1-1 against Egypt, who fought back to equalise and almost managed to win … so all this left England's manager pondering just how good – or fortunate – the opposition had been. Shilton's 120th appearance would set a new record as he overtook Pat Jennings' tally, but England had several players nursing injuries and stand-in 'keeper David Seaman (who had broken a thumb in training) was replaced by Dave Beasant, who flew out at a minute's notice. Robson's calculations were upset soon after the kick-off, as he saw the Dutch team formation – he had decided to use a sweeper, and he had guessed wrongly. However, he quickly made adjustments, switching Butcher to right-back, and he got the response he needed.

Both teams appeared to have raised their game, after their initial outings in the tournament, and the football flowed. However, skipper Robson had to retire in the second half, so David Platt was sent on, while Bull replaced Waddle with 30 minutes to go. As it turned out, the players on each side cancelled each other out, although there were near-misses and plenty of thrills and spills. By the end of the 90 minutes, though, neither side had managed a goal … which meant that England, with two points, now needed to draw with Egypt to go through to the later stages. Naturally, they wanted to hit a high note and beat the Egyptians, not least because that way they would head their group and take the easier route to the finals. In the event, as the Republic drew with Egypt, all four teams were level, and if it worked out that England and Egypt drew and the Republic and the Dutch drew, by the same score, then they would all have to draw lots to decide who played whom and which team was eliminated.

As England headed for their confrontation with the Egyptians, Robson the manager had injury worries about Robson the player, and about Lineker, who had a very sore toe. Bryan Robson had Achilles-tendon problems, Lineker was unable to train. Eventually, the story broke that England's skipper was seeing a faith healer who had helped him before, in the bid to get the injury sorted out. It was a last, desperate effort.

The decision was taken in the end that Robson and Butcher would not play, while Bull and McMahon would. Another player sidelined was Beardsley, though he was to figure as a substitute during the action. Meanwhile, the story of the faith healer had broken, and the tabloids made the most of it. By this time Scotland were out of the tournament, having lost 1-0 to Brazil, and so were Sweden, beaten by Costa Rica after having been ahead – which all went to show that you could profit by expecting anything to happen in this World Cup. It had been that way, so far, and England couldn't afford to be complacent against Egypt ... although they did gamble on playing Lineker from the start. And he managed to last the 90 minutes. Even so, the Egyptians took some breaking down, and it was a goal from a defender, Mark Wright, which settled the issue, just inside the hour. That was the only score, and the result meant that England topped their group. The Republic of Ireland? – They had drawn with Holland, so it came down to drawing lots for them, and the end result was that the Irish took second spot while the Dutch had to face West Germany. As for England, they were up against Belgium in Bologna.

Before that match, Bryan Robson had one last go at making a recovery – it was all in vain – while Shilton confided to his manager that once England had finished with this World Cup, he would be bowing out of the international arena. By then he had reached the age of 40. Overall, the tournament was taking its final shape ... Costa Rica were now out, Cameroon were through to the last eight and, if England did the business against the Belgians, they would be facing the Africans (Roger Milla and all) in the quarter-finals. Brazil, too, had gone out – beaten by Argentina. As for Bryan Robson, he had flown home to see an orthopaedic surgeon. Meanwhile, Robson the manager was being briefed by his spies on the Belgians, and seeing for himself on tape as Belgium played Uruguay. His team-selection posers still had to be solved, and at that stage McMahon was in from the start again, as was Wright. So was Lineker, despite his injury problem. Dave Sexton and John Lyall were the men deputed to mark England's card about the Belgians, and they did a good job ... although, on the day, their goalkeeper played out of his skin. Overall, though, this was another match which gave Bobby Robson cause for great satisfaction, as it ended with a 1-0 victory.

There was general agreement that this was an excellent game, played in the right spirit and containing its fair share of drama – not least , because it was balanced on a knife-edge right to the end. It took not 90 minutes, but 119 minutes for a goal to be scored ... and the marksman was a player who was to plunder goals more and more, as he forced his way into the side as a regular and took over the captaincy. David Platt. Remember? – He was the youngster freed by Manchester United and who, finally, returned from Italy to English football with Arsenal, after having cost a grand total of £22 million in transfer fees...

The game against Belgium see-sawed; and the first strike went to England's opponents – as they hit the woodwork. Shilton was called upon to make two fine saves, as well, then John Barnes had what seemed to be a good goal disallowed for offside. Belgium hit the woodwork for a second time, and the longer the game went on it seemed that the side which could break the deadlock would emerge as the winners. There were 20 minutes still to go when Platt replaced McMahon, who had done a good job but run himself almost to a standstill. Meanwhile, Barnes seemed to be suffering from groin trouble and Lineker was clearly in pain with his toe, once the effects of the injection had begun to wear off. Still, Waddle was presenting a threat to the opposition every time he got the ball, and when Bull replaced Barnes he almost scored straight away.

As the game wore on, Walker and Butcher joined the England casualty list, and with extra time looming it was a matter of holding on. England now had to rely upon their substitutes showing the rest of the team the way … they were still fresh, and they were required to give the lead. The 90 minutes ended and the extra period began – and with it, the strain began to tell on all the players, both from a mental point of view, as well as physically. Tired legs could barely cope, and as Gascoigne managed to make yet another surge forward, he was felled by Gerets, who seemed to be shattered. That was the moment England made the breakthrough, as Gascoigne curled the free-kick over, and Platt timed his run to perfection, as he has done so often in the cause of his country. He was spot-on as he volleyed the ball home in spectacular fashion. That goal was the match-winner, because the Belgians could scarcely get back into the game, since 119 minutes had gone by.

So England were through to the quarter-finals and facing the once-unrated outsiders of Cameroon; but Cameroon had indeed come a long way since their arrival on the World Cup stage. Now, as everyone realised, they could not be taken lightly. For England, it was on from Bologna to Naples, and while they must meet Cameroon, the other quarter-finalists were also emerging … Yugoslavia, for instance, who had beaten Spain; and, of course, the West Germans, along with the host nations Italy. Cameroon had one advantage, right at the start – they had eight days free before the battle, while England must tackle them after five days – and one of those days had been spent travelling. The England hotel was up in the hills, above Salerno (scene of an epic battle during world war two) … down in Naples, it was like an oven. What did they say? – See Naples and die…

Bobby Robson, as usual, had his injury worries. Barnes, Walker, Lineker – the last-named was still forced to rest most of the time between matches, so sore was his toe. When England went for a training session in Naples on the last day of June, the temperature was in the 90's, and when Robson came to the matter of team selection, Platt was in, McMahon was out. Barnes and Lineker? – Both these potential match-winners were in the line-up from the start. Wright's groin injury was a worry but in the event he, too, made it, as did Butcher, who was named captain. On the eve of the match, there was another quarter-final being played, and the result was that Argentina managed to deliver the knock-out blow to the impressive Yugoslavia in a penalty shoot-out. It had been 0-0 after 90 minutes, and the shoot-out (in which Maradona missed his spot-kick) ended 3-2 for Argentina. Meanwhile, Jack Charlton's Republic of Ireland did themselves proud in the battle with Italy, who just managed to have the edge thanks to a goal from their new scoring idol, Toto Schillaci.

So the scene was set for the showdown against Cameroon, and the news from home was that Bryan Robson would not be returning; instead, he had undergone surgery. At the England team's headquarters, manager Robson studied Howard Wilkinson's report on Cameroon, along with reports from John Lyall and Mick Wadsworth. One tip from Wilkinson was that Cameroon would try to slow the game down, not least by time-wasting – therefore, England should force the pace. Even so, and despite the fact that Milla was 38, he could go like the wind.

Milla had gone on and done great damage to other teams, and he had raised the spirits of his own team-mates. His scoring record alone showed that he would need careful watching. As it turned out, however, he had to bide his time. And while England still had to remain wary, Cameroon also had their problems, since four of their squad were ineligible through suspension. Even before the match, England knew whom they would meet in the semi-finals, should they win the duel with Cameroon – it would be West Germany, the old enemy from Wembley in 1966. They had ended the interest of the Czechs in the afternoon match.

One of the things England had to counter was the support Cameroon were being given – they had made themselves great favourites with just about everyone, and they were cheered on by anyone who wasn't English. They went at Robson's team from the start, and it took a fine save from Shilton to deny Omam Biyik a goal. Then it was England's turn to drive forward, and this attack did result in a goal, as Platt, boring through, got on to the end of a cross from Pearce. After that, however, it was all Cameroon as they attacked and gave the England defenders a hard time of it. In fact, England's display after the goal had their manager giving his players some hard words at half-time, with a warning that if they didn't pull their socks up, they would find themselves failing to reach the semi-finals.

Barnes was finding that his injury was playing him up, and with the second half no more than a minute old it was the signal for him to be replaced by Beardsley, while with around quarter of an hour to go, Butcher was hauled off and Steven joined the fray. Added to that, there were two penalty decisions which turned out to be crucial … one against England, the other against Cameroon. When Platt was brought down by the 'keeper, the Mexican referee simply waved play on, but when Milla went down under a challenge from Gascoigne, the spot-kick was awarded, and Kunde made no mistake. England's players reckoned that Milla had kidded the referee, but they couldn't reverse that goal. And inside five minutes. Cameroon were leading, as Ekeke, who had been on the field only 60 seconds, took a pass from Milla and did the business. Then Biyik went close to making it 3-1, and while the Cameroon supporters went almost delirious with delight, the England fans were reduced to silence and Robson began to fear the worst.

It was Gascoigne who finally started the England revival – although, when Wright received an eye injury, it seemed as if the fates were against England. But the players battled on … none more than the defender, who refused to cry quits even though his eye was closed. With Walker limping and obviously feeling the strain, and England's two substitutes already on the field, it was a time for drastic remedies, so Wright was given the nod to go back on and try to see (try being the operative word) what he could do. Even before then, England had seen a scoring opportunity go by, as Gascoigne produced a defence-splitting pass which Platt – who else? – latched on to. But as he beat the Cameroon 'keeper, he saw the ball slide agonizingly past the outside of the post.

The return of Wright, plus the emergence of Gascoigne as a player of influence, helped to give every other England man real heart, and suddenly Cameroon knew they had a fight on their hands. Gascoigne produced another telling through ball, Lineker forgot his sore toe as he chased the ball – and then he was being downed in the area. Penalty! No more than eight minutes to the final whistle, and all to play for, as Lineker dusted himself down and got on with the job. He took the spot-kick himself and the ball went straight into the net. Now it was a match with overtones of the 1966 World Cup final at Wembley, the difference being that this time it was England who had pulled the chestnuts out of the fire.

The question, of course, was whether or not they had shot their bolt in their efforts to produce an equaliser. They still had to cope with the conditions, as well as the opposition – and they had to manage it for another 30 minutes. It was time for a clarion call from the manager and, as Ramsey had done in 1966, so Robson did the same now as he demanded one last effort and asked his players if they really did want to win the match. They responded in style, and as time went by it started to become clear which team had their tails up. When the next goal came, it came from the penalty spot once more – and it was a penalty awarded to England. Robson's players had been awarded only a couple of spot-kicks during the eight years he had been manager; now, in the space of less than half an hour, he had seen his side awarded two penalties. And the second followed the pattern of the first, as Lineker was felled, then he picked himself up and drilled the ball home, to make the score 3-2.

The victory meant that in three days' time, England faced a semi-final with West Germany, and immediately there was concern over whether or not Wright would be fit to play, in view of that horrendous eye injury. Once again, England were on their travels, this time to the city of Turin, and no-one doubted the quality of the opposition the West Germans represented – indeed the winners of this one could well end up taking the World Cup home. The first semi-final ended with tears for the host nation, Italy, and the Argentinians moving (somewhat luckily) into their third final in a dozen years. Maradona and his mates had now become the second favourites to win the trophy – and they didn't even know if they would be facing England or West

Germany.

The Germans had an ace in Lothar Matthaus, who had emerged as the best player in the tournament; on the other hand, England had the unpredictable genius of Gascoigne and the rapidly-maturing Platt. Still, Matthaus wasn't the only big gun in Germany's armoury ... they also had Jurgen Klinsmann and Rudi Voller, though the latter was substituted after having suffered an injury. However, when the whistle went for half-time there was still no score, but as the teams walked off the pitch the applause demonstrated the kind of football which had been served up for the fans to savour. The Germans came out as if determined to run the show, and for quarter of an hour they were undoubtedly in control – so much so that they went into the lead.

The referee awarded a free-kick after he ruled that Pearce had fouled Hassler, and when Andreas Brehme took the kick, he also earned his side a massive slice of luck. As the ball went forward, it met the foot of Paul Parker, and it was deflected from the England man's boot, to catch Shilton coming off his line. He had little or no chance with the deflection, as the ball sped past him and went in just under the bar. England 0 West Germany 1 ... but still Robson's men were not out of the competition, even if they were temporarily down. That was when their manager took off Butcher, sent on Steven and switched Waddle to the wing. His bold gamble succeeded – and it was the unfortunate Parker who played a crucial role once more, this time as he sent the ball into the Germans' 18-yard box. Three of them were there, but between them they failed to do anything as Lineker gained possession, wove a way through and beat 'keeper Illgner.

Ten minutes left, and it was now 1-1; and that was how the scoreline stayed, as extra time became a certainty. Once again, there was an echo of the 1966 final as Robson reminded his players that they could still do it, if they showed the right attitude ... after all, they had gone through all this twice before and come through safely. Still the game ebbed and flowed; Waddle's shot hit the inside of a post and rebounded, Buchwald's effort struck the outside of a post, and Shilton, as ever, was safe as houses in making magnificent saves to foil Matthaus and Klinsmann. Yet the most memorable moment of that extra period came when Gascoigne, having comitted a foul with a mistimed challenge on Berthold, was handed his second caution of the tournament. It meant that, should England reach the final, he would be no more than an onlooker. So the tears flowed, and the watching world saw, via television, the effect this knowledge had on the England player, as he lifted his shirt to wipe away those tears.

In the end, there were no more goals and it was down to a penalty shoot-out; one which the Germans won. England's plan, should a shoot-out become necessary, was for Lineker to strike the first blow and Pearce to step up for spot-kick No. 4 – the one which, in Robson's eyes, was the vital one ... especially if your side had already failed with one. In those circumstances, the opposition knew they still had to make certain with their final shot. England, having won the toss, put Lineker in to bat, so to speak, and he clipped the ball past Illgner. Brehme followed suit by beating Shilton, Beardsley gave England the edge again, then Matthaus levelled matters. Platt stepped up – and scored; so did Riedel, who had gone on as substitute for Voller. Three-all, and Pearce to take that crucial fourth spot-kick. He placed the ball, walked back a few paces, ran forward and drove the ball goalwards … only to see Illgner make the save with his feet. The next man in for Germany was Thon, and he beat Shilton, leaving Waddle to make up the deficit – if he could. Waddle placed the ball, walked back, ran forward … and ballooned the ball in such a fashion that the Germans realised then that they need not even bother taking their fifth spot-kick. So West Germany went through to meet Argentina, England were left with the formality of meeting Italy in the third-fourth-place battle, and the World Cup was over for Bobby Robson and his players. For Robson, in fact, it was the semi-final straw, because he was making his exit … for good.

Through eight years he had worked and striven, suffered the taunts of those who were not slow to deride, and finished up knowing, even before the 1990 World Cup finals, that no matter what, he would become England's ex-manager. Amazingly, or so it seemed, for the first time he was not being criticized in the face of a defeat. In fact, it had been one month exactly before the World Cup kicked off in Italy that Robson had known his fate. He had lived in hopes that his bosses would tell him they were keen for him to stay on, but it hadn't happened; so he had decided to take up the offer from PSV Eindhoven in Holland, and return to club management. Remarkably, Robson learned from a newspaper source that his successor would be Graham Taylor – and this before the news had been officially confirmed that he would be bowing out after Italia '90. Not surprisingly, Robson – having been told by FA chairman Sir Bert Millichip that he could give no guarantees about his future – felt obliged to listen to what PSV had to say, and that was that. He made his exit, Graham Taylor took up the challenge – and, maybe, in many ways he lived to regret it.

CHAPTER 12

SIR ALF RAMSEY, born at Five Elms Farm, Dagenham, was the son of a hay-and-straw dealer; Graham Taylor, too, was born at a farm – in Worksop – but his Dad became a sports journalist at Scunthorpe, where the family had moved a couple of years after Graham's arrival in September, 1944. Graham Taylor and I have something in common – we both got to know a trio of managers rather well ... Dick Duckworth (who was the team boss at Scunthorpe), Jim Smith (who teamed up with Taylor at Lincoln City), and Jimmy McGuigan (a Scot who managed Grimsby Town and who, according to the man who managed England during the 1990's, became one of the most influential people in his footballing life). When Scunthorpe played at the Old Show Ground, I used to drive across from Manchester to see Dick Duckworth, whom I also knew well as the manager of Stockport County. I never met Graham Taylor then, because while he did some training with the Scunthorpe players during school holidays, he never got the chance to play for the club – instead, he joined Grimsby Town, then managed by Tim Ward.

Taylor did play for Scunthorpe Boys, for the England Under-15 side, for Lincolnshire Grammar Schools and for the England Under-19 side, so it wasn't surprising that he envisaged a future in football. He was in a bit of a hurry, too, since he left school without having taken A-level exams; but, despite the names the tabloids called him later, he was never short of brains. When he was managing Watford and Aston Villa, I always found him easy to approach for an after-match quote ... no doubt his experience of the newspaper business during his early years had helped him to recognize that we all have a job to do ... even though he was made to suffer from media attention and attacks later.

When Graham Taylor joined Grimsby Town in the summer of 1962, they had just been promoted to the Second Division – but their manager was on the verge of moving to Derby County. Tim Ward decided against doing a bit of managerial poaching, so Taylor stayed at Blundell Park, as he pondered on advice from the man who had so recently signed him. 'You only get out of the game what you put into it'. Those words must have made him ponder some more, during the 1990's, as he made his exit not only from the England job, but from Wolverhampton Wanderers. Taylor himself admitted that when he left the grammar school, where 'it was three cheers for the opposition at the end of the game', he was not equipped for the atmosphere of the professional game. He found it 'selfish', and swiftly realised that 'you had to look after yourself'.

Taylor's debut for Grimsby Town was on his 18th birthday, against Newcastle United; later, he found he was one of 10 wing-halves on the books, and he had to adapt to playing at full-back. He admitted that in later years it rankled when he was regarded merely as a lower-division player. 'I was lucky to get a career out of the game… I think that was a credit to my ability'. And before he had finished he had totalled close on 400 appearances 'in a position I had had to teach myself '. After two terms in the Second Division, Grimsby fell from grace, relegated on goal average at the end of season 1963-64. That was when Jimmy McGuigan entered Graham Taylor's footballing life – under him, Taylor became captain and, indeed, the youngest qualified coach of his generation. McGuigan taught him that while football was a simple game, 'there were things you could appreciate and do off the ball, as well as on it. He taught us to work as a team, explained that we all had a part to play as individuals within that team'. McGuigan was later to be asked to go on scouting missions, as Taylor managed Watford, then Aston Villa.

Like Graham Taylor, I have a fond memory of Jimmy McGuigan, if for a very different reason – because it was Jimmy who introduced me to the benefits of a drop of Scotch. Previously, I had drunk only cream sherry … one day, when I went to see Jimmy at his club, there was no sherry, and he persuaded me to take a 'wee dram'. I still enjoy a drop of Scotch … in moderation, of course. That first day, after my initiation, however, my feet hardly seemed to touch the ground as I swayed out of Jimmy's office.

In time, McGuigan left Grimsby; and so did Taylor. He had done five years there, then he moved to Fourth Division Lincoln City, where he became a team-mate of Jim Smith and Ray Harford. When Jim became manager of Colchester United, he signed Harford – 'a big, strapping centre-half' – whose playing career took in a 12-year spell with half a dozen clubs before management beckoned, at Fulham, Luton Town, Wimbledon and Blackburn Rovers. Harford was to join forces for a while with Taylor when the latter was England team boss. Back in November, 1972, however, it was a step up for Graham Taylor when, before he had reached the age of 30, he was asked to combine the jobs of playing and managing at Lincoln. The next seven games ended with two defeats and five draws and, for the first (but not the last) time Taylor heard cries for his dismissal from irate supporters. But the board stood firm, results got better, and Lincoln finished in 10th place.

During the next couple of years, Taylor turned over the playing personnel and Lincoln stayed in mid-table; then they began their climb. One key man was centre-half Sam Ellis, who as a 19-year-old had played for Sheffield Wednesday against Everton in the 1966 final of the FA Cup. After spells on the backroom side at places such as Blackpool, Bury and Manchester City, he returned to Lincoln as team boss in the mid-1990's. Ellis came to admire Taylor and his way of doing things, and he reckoned that in addition to producing a winning team at Sincil Bank, the young manager demonstrated the art of public relations, as he developed a family atmosphere at the club. So much so that the signing of 'keeper Peter Grotier came about because the fans themselves chipped in £16,000 of the £20,000 fee, from charity walks and other fund-raising efforts.

By the end of the season, Lincoln were heading the Fourth Division; they had scored 111 goals and totalled 74 points – a record haul. And for a while they threatened to surge to the top of the Third Division, although they finally had to settle for eighth place. By the spring of 1977, Graham Taylor was being asked to consider making a move to West Brom, who were promising to make a genuine challenge for the championship. However, when Taylor and the Albion directors got down to some straight talking, he gave them the thumbs-down ... then, surprisingly to most onlookers of the game, inside a couple of months he was accepting a job back in the Fourth Division, with Watford.

There were those who reckoned that Taylor knew his limitations, hence his decision not to take up the challenge of rnanaging a club in the top flight; after all, he had taken Lincoln out of the fourth, and so he could reasonably expect to do well at another club in that league, especially since he was being backed by showbiz star Elton John. Yet, as he said himself, what Taylor was looking for was control, 'the power to give myself the chance to be successful'. And, as he also said, at Watford he would stand or fall by his own efforts, because Elton John had told him to get on with managing the club ... 'that's what I pay you for'. It was John' s ambition to see Watford break through to the First Division and go into Europe, and with Taylor as manager and the pop star providing the wherewithal, the opportunity was there – even though it did cost more than the £1 million Taylor had warned it would cost, for starters.

In fact, Taylor did point out that while Elton John invested cash for signings on three occasions, all the other money went into developing the ground at Vicarage Road. However, when it came to the backroom side, Taylor wanted a man with top-flight experience, and he persuaded Bertie Mee to become assistant manager. Mee had steered Arsenal to the double at the start of the 1970's, but he was not taking any active part in the game when Taylor talked to him. There was another recruit, too – Sam Ellis, who was to declare that when it came to taking a club out of the bottom league, Taylor plumped for experience, rather than raw youth. The youngsters – and there were quite a few groomed at Watford – appeared on the scene later; names like Kenny Jackett, Steve Terry and Les Taylor became familiar, along with one who went all the way to the top, with Liverpool and England, John Barnes.

It was Barnes who told me how he was spotted while playing for a side called Sudbury Court, in the Middlesex League, and he was to bring Watford the best part of £1 million when he left for Anfield. Two other players to make their mark with Watford were winger Nigel Callaghan and striker Luther Blissett, who would move into Italian football for big money. By 1996, Taylor, Jackett and Blissett were back at Vicarage Road, striving to halt Watford's slide into the Second Division. But the first

Graham Taylor who was successful as a League manager but failed to take England to the 1994 World Cup Finals.

time round it was exciting, as the club climbed out of the Fourth Division at the end of Taylor's first season. They led the way by 11 points.

Taylor himself declared that he hadn't gone to Watford merely to win another Fourth Division championship... Bertie Mee's value lay in the fact that he was the man who knew all about football in the top flight. And that was where Taylor and Watford were heading. The Vicarage Road club followed up by winning promotion again, and while Watford finished down in 18th place, valuable lessons had been learned by the end of the season. According to Sam Ellis, Taylor concentrated on preparing his own side, rather than on what the opposition might do, and certainly the manager's methods paid dividends, as Watford moved up the table in the Second Division. Season 1979-80 saw them finish ninth, and by the spring of 1982 they were on their way into the top flight – and, for good measure, they carried off the prestigious FA Youth Cup. By that time, the youth policy was paying off handsomely, while close on £1,000,000 came in through season-ticket sales and sponsorship.

Taylor declared publicly that he wasn't keen about delving into the transfer market and splashing out ... 'when you start talking millions of pounds it takes the thing completely out of proportion'. During his later days, at Aston Villa, he was to snap up David Platt from Crewe Alexandra for around £200,000 – and by the time Platt was with Arsenal in 1996, his transfer fees overall had soared to £22 million. Sam Ellis said that while Taylor listened to his players, 'they did as they were told'. And when Watford kicked off in the First Division, they raised a few eyebrows as they beat Everton 2-0 at home and Southampton 4-1 away. In fact, there were three victories in the first five outings, and after Watford had been put in their place (or so it seemed) by Nottingham Forest, in the last week of September they staggered everyone by demolishing Sunderland, with an 8-0 romp at Vicarage Road. That game saw Blissett strike his first hat-trick for the club he had joined as a schoolboy, in 1974.

People simply had to take notice, not only because of the result, but because the victory hoisted Watford into third place, behind the expected pacemakers, Manchester United and Liverpool. On a personal level, Taylor was rewarded by being asked to take charge of the England youth squad, although some critics wondered out loud if the way Watford played was the way forward at international level. It was a school of thought which was given voice again during Taylor's days in charge of the senior England side.

More than once, Taylor was to refute the charge that he was obsessed with 'long-ball' tactics, and after a match in which Watford beat Tottenham Hotspur 1-0 at White Hart Lane, their debut in the country's capital city became the occasion for some vitriolic criticism to be levelled at their style of play. Then Watford beat Arsenal 4-2 at Highbury, and it became clear that no matter what the critics said, Taylor's team must be taken seriously as challengers for honours. At the half-way stage they were still third from top, and while some wondered it they would turn out to be one-season wonders, Taylor and his team simply carried on, regardless. Liverpool were always going to finish ahead of the pack, and they ended up with an 11-point lead; but it was Watford, not Manchester United, who chased them hone, as they rounded off a season in which they had won 22 matches.

Their final game was against Liverpool, at Vicarage Road, and Bob Paisley had already taken his seat in the stand at Anfield for the last time as manager of the club he had served for more than 40 years. He had taken his bow as Liverpool beat Aston Villa to celebrate yet another title success, and now he was bowing out at Vicarage Road. Liverpool had beaten Watford 3-1 at Anfield in mid-December, but Taylor's side gained revenge in mid-May, with a 2-1 victory, and he kept the team sheet from the match. That win gave Watford's manager tremendous satisfaction, not least because 'if there was a man I did admire from a distance, it was Bob Paisley'. So Watford were with the big boys in Europe, but they sold Blissett to AC Milan for almost £1 million – which meant that they could not count on getting another 27 goals in a season from their ace marksman. Even so, they did not give in.

Against their first European opponents, Kaiserslautern, they lost 3-1 in Germany but won the return 3-0, to take on the Bulgarian side, Levski Spartak. Despite missing a penalty and being held to a 1-1 draw, they took the return game to extra time and emerged as 3-1 victors. The next two outings, against Sparta Prague, were to see the end of Watford's European dreams, as the Czechs won 3-2 at Vicarage Road and 4-0 on home territory. But if Watford were out of Europe, they took another route to success as they made their mark in the FA Cup, beating Luton Town, Charlton Athletic, Brighton and Birmingham City, to go through to the semi-finals. So far the opposition had been rated as no great shakes, and in the penultimate round they were paired with Third Division Plymouth Argyle.

Naturally, Watford were expected to win, and they did; but by the only goal of the game. Now, people said, let's see what they can do against top-class opposition ... which came from Howard Kendall's Everton. Watford had been affected by injury and suspension, and possibly Taylor sensed even before the game began that it was going to end in bitter disappointment for himself and his players. At half-time Everton led 1-0, and when they scored again that was enough to end the final as a competitive match. As Taylor acknowledged later: 'When it's all over, people only want to know the winners'. An echo of what one-time Leeds United chairman Harry Reynolds used to say, that 'you get nowt for being second'.

If others had criticised the Watford style of play, Elton John and his co-directors had no complaints – indeed, Taylor signed on for six more years, in the spring of 1984. He also re-signed Luther Blissett from AC Milan that summer in a cut-price deal, and the next three years were to see Watford consolidate their place in the top flight. Along the way, Watford enhanced their reputation as doughty, FA Cup fighters, and in 1986 Liverpool were somewhat lucky to win their quarter-final tie as they went on to claim the classic double. But all good things come to an end, and for Watford the end came with the departure of Graham Taylor – who took on the job of restoring Aston Villa's faded fortunes.

Villa had suffered relegation, and it was Taylor's task to get them back into the First Division. He was to admit that, after having had severe doubts as to whether or not he had made the right decision in the first place (to leave Watford after his 10-year stint there), he spent his first six months at Villa Park in a constant sweat. According to Taylor, Villa were heading towards the Third Division, rather than poised for an assault on the First. He made several signings, and by the turn of the year Villa had hit the top, despite erratic results on home ground. On the final day of the season there was everything to play for – and not just for Aston Villa. Middlesbrough and Bradford were involved, both teams were playing at home – and both lost. Meanwhile, Villa needed one point from their game against Swindon Town, to claim an automatic promotion spot. They finished up celebrating promotion, just as Watford were taking the drop ... and yet, even as Aston Villa were striving to do better than merely survive, their manager was talking about leaving.

What he said was this: 'I've no intention of staying here for 10 years... I'm looking to get as much done as possible in four years. Whatever we do during the next three years, I don't expect to be manager of Aston Villa after 1992. If I can leave Villa in a position where somebody can take them on to attack the championship, that's fine. If we could do that in the next two years, great – but, whatever happens, I'm looking to other things'. He recalled that when he turned down West Brom and went to Watford, people had accused him of lacking ambition and said he couldn't handle First Division and international players. He called that 'a lot of rubbish'. Taylor also talked about 'other things outside football management', and 'things in football that don't involve team management'. He declared, without equivocation, that 'I'm not going to be a football manager for the rest of my life'. By 1996, he was taking charge again at Watford, though on a somewhat different basis from the first time round … and in between his two spells at Vicarage Road, he had suffered the slings and arrows of managerial misfortune both as manager of the England-international side, and of Wolves.

Even as he was endeavouring to get Aston Villa back on an even keel in the top flight, there was talk that he could be a candidate for the England job, once Bobby Robson stepped down. That day duly arrived after Robson had gone close to success in the 1990 World Cup. Four years on, and Graham Taylor's name was being bandied about as the man who had failed to steer England into the finals in the United States. Between 1990 and 1994, a lot of water flowed under the international footballing bridge, and Graham Taylor was all but drowned in the waves of criticism which were hurled at him. By August, 1993, one eminent journalist was writing that 'the bruised but unbowed Taylor may have only a month left as England's manager – or, if the most recent precedent is followed, he could be returning from America next July a hero of his time. Such is the fickle nature of a life in football'. Taylor then was being urged to take the plunge and 'go for broke' without the mercurial talents of Paul Gascoigne, whose previous two displays, in Poland and Norway, had been 'stunningly anonymous'. And there was more…

San Marino, the no-hopers of the qualifying rounds involving England, would be the final opposition in November, 1993 … 'the last of England's World Cup matches on the treadmill of qualification which has stretched across the past year and driven the country's relationship with Taylor to exasperating limits.' It was further recorded that those who maintained England would reach the finals could well be so wrong – 'that suggests we have left our hold on reality somewhere between Oslo and Foxboro in June, when the threads of an England team at unease with itself were picked bare, first by Norway, then by the United States'. England, in the group with Norway, Holland, Poland, Turkey and San Marino, had suffered defeat on a trip to the United States which brought back memories of that day at Belo Horizonte many years previously. As for Norway, they had proved a task too far for Taylor's team … after seven matches, they led the group with a dozen points, while England stood in second place, three points adrift. Holland, in third place, also had nine points, while Poland had eight points – but two games in hand. Turkey and San Marino were out of it, each having played eight matches and garnered three points and one point, respectively.

Norway had battered San Marino 10-0 and 2-0, beaten Holland 2-1, drawn 1-1 with England at Wembley and defeated England 2-0 in Oslo. They had also held the Dutch to a scoreless draw in Holland. England? – They had beaten San Marino 6-0 (as had the Dutch), defeated Turkey 4-0 and won 2-0 on Turkish soil, while at Wembley England had let the Dutch off the hook by drawing 2-2. The remaining key games for Taylor's team were against Poland at Wembley, against the Dutch in Holland, and against San Marino in the tiny principality. One writer was offering this view: 'Let's hope it doesn't come down to goal difference and we need a round half-dozen (against San Marino) to qualify, because the the nerves wouldn't stand it'. One point made, tongue in cheek, was that at a recent by-election a 'Sack Graham Taylor' candidate had received 80 votes, desmonstrating that 'the inhabitants of one street, at least, were tempted to register their protest at Taylor's handling of team affairs'. It was recorded: 'Three games from now, we'll know if a handful of Dorset voters reflect the mood of the entire nation'. Taylor, it was said, 'has made it plain that the moment England's task is rendered impossible, he will take leave of a job which has become increasingly wearisome for him'.

CHAPTER 13

IN THE beginning, the Football Association decided that Graham Taylor was the man who should succeed Bobby Robson – after having whittled down the list of names to three ... Howard Kendall, Joe Royle and Taylor ... the man in charge at Aston Villa was the right man for the job. The committee considering the names consisted of Sir Bert Millichip, chairman of the Football Association, Dick Wragg, League-president Bill Fox, Arthur McMullen, Graham Kelly and Peter Swales. Millichip had no doubts; he soon made it clear where his vote would go – to Graham Taylor; and the task was made that much easier when the other two candidates pulled out.

Howard Kendall, in doing so, eased the mind of his chairman, Peter Swales, by indicating that he would prefer to remain in charge of team affairs at Manchester City (though later he did depart for his first love, Everton). Joe Royle told me later: 'I was invited to be interviewed, and felt flattered that my name had come up for consideration; but in the end, I didn't think it was worth going in for the job, at that time. I didn't feel I was ready for it. I was a Second Division manager (with Oldham Athletic); we hadn't won anything; and, in any case, I wasn't ready to give up the day-to-day involvement that you get when you're a club manager. So I wrote back and declined the invitation ... while indicating that if such an opportunity should come up again at a later stage, then the situation might well be different, from my point of view'. In the event, then, all this left Graham Taylor very much as the man on the committee's mind.

So they got Taylor in, and when they had talked to him, they came to the same conclusion as Sir Bert Millichip – even if it meant that the Football Association had to pay Aston Villa compensation of £225,000 for having lost a manager whose contract still had a year to run. At the age of 45, then, Graham Taylor was handed a contract for four years and the responsibility for bringing success to England in the international arena. For the first time in its long history, the Football Association had forked out what amounted to a transfer fee to get their man, and now the jackpot question was: could he deliver?

The answer became apparent, as England's players and their manager floundered in their efforts to achieve their goal – the finals of the World Cup in the United States in 1994 ... in fact, they didn't even reach their hoped-for destination. Yet, even as Taylor was striving – and struggling – to get his team back on the rails, Peter Swales was still maintaining that he was 'the right man for the job' – a viewpoint, it must be admitted, which was not shared by everyone in the football world. Sir Bobby Charlton, for instance – after the match against Norway had ended in what could fairly be described as a disaster, this World Cup winner of 1966 was taking a totally different line to Swales ... like this: 'We were technically naive, unprofessional in everything we did. It was a performance that really plumbed the depths'. For the man whose name was synonymous with Manchester United, as well as England, this kind of biting criticism was somewhat unusual. As he said: 'What really hurts a lot of people is not that they lost the match, but the way they lost it. We always seem to pride ourselves on being aggressive, tough, professional and brave.' But on this occasion, 'those were all the qualities we were lacking' .

Swales still stood by his man as he said: 'We have three matches left ... it's still feasible that we might qualify'. And later, after it had all gone wrong, Swales stood accused by his critics of having said that England would qualify 'easily' for the 1994 World Cup finals. He also stood accused of having declared that when England went no further than the semi-finals in Italy, in 1990, it might have been a blessing in disguise. And, of course, there was the long-standing argument over Jack Charlton, who claimed he had never even been given an interview when he had once applied for the job of being England's team boss. Swales told me that 'they all looked good bets when they got the job', and in the case of Bobby Robson he insisted that he had been misunderstood about his 'blessing in disguise' remark.

Swales: 'I didn't actually say that. I said I felt we needed a new face in the job; a fresh face. So from that point of view it was probably a good job that he didn't succeed in taking England all the way. I wasn't knocking Bobby as much as saying we needed a fresh face. His record now says he was better than Graham Taylor ... I thought Graham had the better potential, but it didn't work out that way. And for my money, yes – we did have a bit of luck in 1990.' Swales again: 'I stuck with Graham Taylor because I thought he could do the job. I don't feel he got the breaks, and the whole thing just turned against him. Yes, we did have our differences of opinion – if you don't have them, you don't have a relationship. And remember that any manager is only as good as his players – I could have managed Brazil and Hungary in their hey-day, and we haven't had the quality of players since 1966.

'The beauty of football, though, is that there is such a fine line between success and failure. Greenwood, Revie, Robson, Taylor ... they all had good track records, and Taylor struck me as being the best. I couldn't tell you why I thought that, just as I couldn't tell you why Revie was a great club manager but a poor England manager. I do know the England job is different to running a club ... it needs someone who is self-opinionated, someone who will do his own thing.'

Swales did admit: 'I suppose Jack Charlton should have been given an interview for the England job... I don't know why he didn't get one. And there are a lot of things you can put right – with hindsight'. When Taylor made his exit from the job at Wolves, one headline recorded that he had been 'Hounded Out', and Wolves' commercial manager, David Clayton, offered the opinion that Taylor 'did not want to put his family through any more pressure ... he had it with England and, if he had stayed, it might have been even more intense at local level? By then, Taylor was 51 years old, and being described as a 'proud, honest but flawed manager'. Phil Neal, who sat at Taylor's shoulder – during those closing matches of his England reign, understood what Taylor had to endure. Phil told me how he saw another manager suffer as the fans at one home game hurled taunts ... 'it was frightening ... there was an atmosphere of real hate'.

While Taylor 'had to live with it' as England manager, in the words of Peter Swales, he also had to live with criticism not just from the men who pen words, but from people inside the game – such as Sir Bobby Charlton and Gary Lineker. For example, when everyone seemed to be backing Chris Waddle for a place as England prepared to take on Holland. When Waddle's name was missing from the team sheet in April, 1993, Charlton expressed 'sheer disbelief' as he declared: 'I can't understand why he isn't being given the chance – I imagine the Dutch will be pleased. Waddle has the type of skills which aren't widespread in our game'.

Lineker was even more forthright. 'I've been saying since I retired that Waddle would be in any side of mine, and so would Peter Beardsley. I don't think age matters, if they're the best players – and, for me, both still are'. Lineker (who had been discarded by Taylor amid great argument, when he was one goal short of equalling Bobby Charlton's 49-goal record for England) termed Waddle's omission 'inconceivable' and claimed it had more to do with a clash of personalities than with football matters. 'I don't believe it's a football issue... I just don't think they really get on. I think it's more of a personality clash – there's no reason, football-wise, why he shouldn't be in the squad. I can understand the manager's argument that he doesn't want to change a winning team; the one thing we need is a steady side. But he would be a nice player to have on the bench.'

On the eve of the match against Poland, one writer was saying: 'Graham Taylor needs no reminding of the irony of England's crucial World Cup qualifier at Wembley on Wednesday. Twenty years ago, on October 17, 1973, England could only draw 1-1 with the Poles, a result that cost them a place in the 1974 World Cup finals in Germany. The 100,000 crowd were witnessing the end of the Ramsey era ... the following spring, Ramsey was sacked'. It was recalled how 'Jan Domarski punished Norman Hunter with a vital, second-half goal' and how, despite Allan Clarke's penalty-goal equalizer, Poland's 'keeper, Jan Tomazewski, 'described by ITV's guest critic, Brian Clough, as "a clown", turned on a wonder show to foil England'. It was further recorded: 'The 12 players Ramsey used on that disastrous night still carry the scars'. They were Peter Shilton, Paul Madeley, Evelyn Hughes, Norman Hunter, Colin Bell, Roy McFarland, Tony Currie, Mick Channon, Martin Chivers, Allan Clarke, Martin Peters and Kevin Hector. When England tried conclusions with Poland at Wembley on September 8, 1993, there were no mistakes – after a 3-0 victory, Taylor's team was in upbeat mood again, and there was optimism about the matches to come, against Holland and in San Marino.

On September 22, it was recorded that the Dutch had scored seven goals against San Marino, while on the eve of the game against Holland, the news was that Graham Taylor had named only three of the players who, the previous April, had drawn 2-2 with the Dutch at Wembley. Taylor was 'unhappily snappy with reporters at the Press conference'. It was a 50,000 sell-out in Rotterdam, and Dutch coach Dick Advocaat had said before the San Marino match: 'We need goals, and nothing less than four points from the two games; if we only draw against England, we are finished'. Advocaat dismissed the Poles – 'I have never rated them in our group. I felt from the start it would be between England and Holland. The surprise was Norway'. He recalled that when Holland drew 2-2 with Poland in Rotterdam, 'we created 15 chances, hit the woodwork four times and should have won easily. England created only seven chances, yet won 3-0'. A former England World Cup manager, Bobby Robson, had words of advice for Graham Taylor: 'Go to Holland to win ... exude confidence within the ranks. In my experience, players can sniff even the faintest hint of anxiety like a pack of foxhounds'. Even so, Robson conceded that a draw in Holland and a win over San Marino would 'do the trick'.

The dreadful reality was that Holland inflicted a 2-0 defeat upon England, as one disaster followed another during the match. Although German referee Karl Josef Assenmacher disallowed a Dutch goal by Frank Rijkaard, he also failed to issue marching orders to the flaxen-haired Ronald Koeman for a professional foul on David Platt. Koeman, a key man in the Dutch side, subsequently scored from a free-kick, to add insult to injury, and that defeat, in effect, sealed Graham Taylor's fate as the manager of England. Taylor later reflected upon the match: 'The ref. got it wrong...' He also talked candidly about the television documentary which, as it was beamed to the nation's millions of viewers, became notorious for the frequent use of the 'F' word. There were also a couple of Taylor phrases which stuck in the memory... 'Do I not like that', and 'You've got me the sack'. Meaning, in the second instance, the referee.

Taylor was to admit: 'I'm not proud to be seen swearing in public, but I'm not hypocritical. It's the language of the environment. The film wasn't made for the media – it was made for the football supporter. What happened was that they suddenly saw this fellow – me – who cared, who used words that they used. I cared passionately. I know I said "You've got me the sack", but it was a comment anyone would have made. That referee got it wrong at a vital time for England, never mind Graham Taylor. And I was expected to sit down? – He never refereed another international, you know. But what good is that now?'

Taylor also confessed that 'my professional pride was hurt... I wanted to be the England manager, and I wanted to be successful'. As he looked back over his turbulent England career, he recalled the calmer days when he managed Watford. One day he received an invitation to visit the home of Vernon Edwards, who at the time was the official medical adviser both for the Vicarage Road club and for England. It was a visit which clearly made an impression upon Taylor … an impression which remained vivid as the years passed by.

The then England manager, Bobby Robson, was there that day, and England had failed to qualify for the European championships. 'I can remember getting home and Rita (Taylor's wife) saying how ill she thought Bobby had looked. There's no doubt I looked just as ill as him by the end'. Like Robson, Taylor suffered the anguish of knowing that his England team hadn't qualified for the European championships, and there had been the controversy over his substitution of striker Gary Lineker in June, 1992, as England went out of the championship against Sweden. There was a cruel headline over that one: Swedes 2, Turnips 1. The caricature of Taylor was not only unkind … 'from that moment, I was the villain … I had rejected the nation's hero'. Yet he argued: 'Gary wasn't playing well, wasn't scoring; and when I look back, where we lost our way in the European championship was in the previous match, against France. We played out a sterile, 1-1 draw. We had beaten them in February – the first defeat France had suffered in three years under Michel Platini – and I hadn't realised the effect that had had on them'.

Taylor recalled that Martin Keown – 'and people ask how did he play for England?' – had man-marked Eric Cantona in both matches 'and he never gave him a kick. What I should have done was made an attempt to win the game … I should have taken Lineker out … he was having a bad time. Then I could have brought him back against Sweden. He had responded positively in such situations, in the past. What irritates me is that people think I took him off in a personal attack. It was a footballing decision – it is often forgotten it was me who appointed him England captain, in the first place'. Lineker, like Sir Bobby Charlton, was to voice his criticism of Taylor's failure to name Chris Waddle in his World Cup squad for the encounter with Holland … and Lineker was also to admit that he never had ambitions about being a manager. 'No-one likes you when you're a manager. The crowd are against you most of the time, and not many managers, I suspect, are happy. It's a job that doesn't appeal to me – I cannot see myself out on the training ground every day, snarling at players to get then going, and having all the moodies'. That wasn't how Graham Taylor felt, though, when he embarked upon management in the international arena. 'We went into the European championships in 1992 with just one defeat from 21 games … we had a group of players who were flexible, and I felt we could do well'.

England didn't do well – and they didn't do well again, when World Cup time came round. The Dutch disaster in Rotterdam occurred on the night of October 13 – unlucky for some! – and the final match was played on November 17. It began in sensational fashion, because San Marino, the sitting ducks for every other nation in their group, scored first against England. Not only that, the goal came after only eight seconds, after Stuart Pearce had delivered a misplaced back-pass. That was the first and last goal England's opponents scored, and Taylor's team recovered to notch seven goals themselves. Even so, this was a last, desperate throw of the dice, and it became clear that the United States would have to do without the 1966 World champions, when it came to the World Cup of 1994. Holland – winners by a 3-1 margin in Poland – and Norway were the nations who made it, while England (in third place and two points adrift of the Dutch) were left to rue the might-have-beens.

Peter Swales had expressed his belief almost to the bitter end that 'we can still qualify', and Graham Kelly, chief executive of the Football Association, had advised that with three games still to go, the requirement was that people should 'sit tight' and await developments. Taylor admitted he had made mistakes – one was when England played in Norway, with Gary Pallister, Tony Adams and Des Walker at the back while Lee Sharpe and Lee Dixon were pushing up on the flanks. 'It didn't come off and, on reflection, I didn't give myself enough time to work on it'. During the final months of Taylor's tenure of office, he was pilloried to a cruel degree, and he confessed that as it became evident England were about to miss out on the 1994 World Cup, 'I was getting the sweats. Even though I'd been asleep, I'd wake up covered in perspiration. It is a sign of being under stress. People who have been under severe strain will understand'. Taylor again: 'For the first 10 days after I resigned as England manager, I would wake up every morning feeling as though I'd gone 10 rounds with Frank Bruno. I ached all over. You have slept – but you're still tired.'

Taylor also said: 'You either go under, or you stick in there and try to maintain as much dignity as you can. But it was only after I resigned as England manager, six days after our final qualifying match against San Marino, that I realized how much stress I'd been under'.

Taylor was to suffer further, when he went back into club management with Wolves. Once again, he found himself under pressure, from the media and from the fans. There was a 0-0 draw against a 10-man Charlton Athletic side, and as hundreds of Wolves supporters demanded that he should go, Taylor made what was termed 'an emotional pledge of loyalty to the Hayward family who run the club'. He said: 'They came and asked me to become manager … it would be totally wrong of me to walk out on them. I have no intention of doing so'. By the afternoon of the following Monday, Taylor had met chairman Jonathan Hayward and been told about the board's concern over team perforances. Wolves had reached the play-offs the previous term, now they languished 15th in the table. And so, two years after having left the England job, Taylor walked out of Molineux. 'He succumbed, as he did then (when his England career ended) to the sheer weight of public opinion against him', it was said.

Not that he went with a whimper – more a statement of defiance for his critics to chew upon. He said 'I am sad, because this has as much to do with matters off the pitch as to those on it'. He had been driving to Molineux when he heard on the car radio that a Press conference had been called to discuss his future. Taylor said: 'I thought to myself, "Do you really need this?"' When, having met the chairman, he was asked to resign, he did so. 'I was more disappointed than bitter. People say my Wolverhampton experience, following England, was another failure. The fact is that in the one full season I had with Wolves – despite an appalling injury list – they missed the Premiership by one game and reached the last eight of the FA Cup, their best year for 12 seasons'.

And then the wheel of football fortune turned full circle, as Elton John persuaded Taylor to return to Watford, this time as general manager. Twice he had failed to respond to such overtures during the previous seven weeks, but 'after I had turned them down for a second time, Elton rang me from Atlanta and asked me to keep my options open until we could meet'. Elton John 'went a long way to convincing me that perhaps I was fighting shy of Watford because I was afraid of how the media would react. I needed someone to say it, rather than me just think it. For the first time, I had come close to chickening out because I was wary of getting hammered in the Press again. I couldn't allow that to happen'.

Taylor then had 18 games in which to salvage First Division survival for the Vicarage Road club, and he would work in tandem with Luther Blissett and Kenny Jackett, two of the men who, as players, had known the glory days with Watford. And even as he looked towards the end of season 1995-96, whatever the outcome of the battle to survive, he reflected upon the wisdom or otherwise of telling his story. He looked at it this way: 'For an autobiography to be worthwhile, it has to be truthful. For my autobiography to be truthful, it's going to hurt people. I'm not certain I want to do that. I've been through that to know what it means'. He did, indeed. As he had said when he left Wolves: 'The team has not been playing well, but only 13 weeks into the season we are still in all competitions, and our recent run of two defeats in 12 games is not as bad as our critics claim. A return of confidence is of prime importance, but a team cannot gain confidence if the board of directors and a section of fans do not have confidence in their manager'. Taylor's record through close on quarter of a century showed that he had been successful from Sincil Bank to Villa Park; but when it came to England, the wheel of football fortune spun in such a manner that he knew he was on a loser.

CHAPTER 14

BRYAN ROBSON talking: 'I know they'll turn on me next for sticking up for Terry, but that doesn't worry me. Someone's got to tell it as it really is. The way they are turning so quickly against Terry, you have to question whether it's possible for anyone to take on this job with a chance of succeeding. No more than 14 months ago, he was the only man for the job. He came in with the 100 per cent support of the public and the Press. His only defeat in 12 games has been by the world champions (Brazil), but all of a sudden, they want him out. The way Terry is being attacked is not only a disgrace, it defies logic. Public opinion is being turned against him by one or two tabloid newspapers who don't think through what they're writing, but for whom the England manager is easy meat for slaughtering articles. It's high time these critics were held accountable, also'. Robson was also dismissive of 'managers and ex-managers who jump on the band-wagon ... they should keep their opinions to themselves and get on with doing their own jobs. I saw the stuff Bobby Robson and Graham Taylor had to suffer ... now it's Terry's turn to take the flak. It's over the top'.

The 'Terry' to whom Bryan Robson referred was, of course, England team-coach Terry Venables, who had been the subject of much controversy – indeed, Venables himself had at one time been engaged in a war of words with an MP who had brought up his name in Parliament. Her name: Kate Hoey. The Venables issue was taken up, too, by Graham Kelly, chief executive of the Football Association, his chairman, Sir Bert Millichip, Noel White, chairman of the international committee, and committee-member Ian Stott.

And while all this was going on, Venables himself – beset by court actions both ongoing and pending – was striving to produce an England team which could win the European championship in the summer of 1996. During the later days of his engagement, Venables declared that 'some people with small minds are making assumptions – they believe I am trying to steamroller through a new contract. That is not the case'. Apart from White, Stott was named as having reservations about a new deal, and about Kelly's authority for negotiating on the matter. Stott said it was 'a key issue' as to whether one man or the whole committee could agree a contract; Kelly hinself admitted that 'a number of issues that have come to light in the two years since we appointed Terry have been greater than we might have expected at the time'. Stott declared that he was 'not anti-Venables... I was seeking to establish the procedure by which he is given an extension to his contract – or whether it is rejected'. Kelly admitted there were 'imponderables flying around'. In the event, Venables decided to bow out, come the end of the European championship, and two 'legal eagles' – Keith Wiseman and Chris Wilcox – were appointed to the sub-committee charged with the task of finding a new England coach, along with White, Millichip and Kelly, though Stott would not be a member of that particular team any longer.

Rarely, if ever, can a football coach have generated as much publicity as Terry Venables. Kate Hoey, the Labour MP for Vauxhall, had asserted in the Commons that Venables was under investigation over allegations that he might have made a 'misleading, false or deceptive' statement in an offer document believed to relate to his purchase of Tottenham Hotspur shares (having left Spurs, Venables became involved in a long-running feud with Tottenham supremo Alan Sugar). In reply to Kate Hoey, Venables claimed there was a campaign to destroy his 'reputation and life' as he said: 'Since leaving Tottenham, I have been the victim of a concerted campaign to discredit me. The allegations are wild and unfounded. For my family, and the families of those close to me, it has been a living nightmare'. Kate Hoey rapped back: 'I am definitely not trying to discredit Mr. Venables'.

From the start, Venables' career in football had been high-profile. Like Sir Alf Ramsey, he was born in Dagenham (on January 6, 1943), and he joined Chelsea as an apprentice in 1958, turning professional two years later. In 202 League games he scored 26 goals; by 1964 he had claimed two England caps (he was capped at all levels); and the following year he was winning a medal in the League Cup. In 1966 – England's World Cup year – he was on his way to Tottenham Hotspur for £80,000, and in 115 League games for Spurs he scored 19 goals. He also picked up an FA Cup-winner's medal in 1967. By 1969 he was on his way to Queen's Park Rangers for a transfer fee of £70,000, and he scored 19 goals as he totalled 179 appearances. By 1974 – the year Ramsey's England reign was summarily ended – Venables was joining Crystal Palace and, as he played only 14 games, coming to the end of that stage of his career. In 1976 he was appointed manager of Palace, and as he steered them out of the Third Division 12 months later and then, in 1979, to the championship of the Second Division, his team were being hailed as the Young Eagles.

By October, 1980 – as Palace occupied a mid-table place in the top flight – Venables was resigning to take charge at Queen's Park Rangers, and two years later they were finishing fifth in Division 2, but reaching the final of the FA Cup. One year on, and Rangers were taking the championship of their division, with Venables becoming managing director and a major shareholder. Come May, 1984, as Rangers stood fifth in Division 1, Venables was joining Barcelona, and the following year they were becoming champions of Spain for the first time in more than a decade. In 1986 Barcelona had to settle for the runners-up spot, but they reached the final of the European Cup, losing in a penalty shoot-out to Steaua Bucharest. Twelve months later, as Barcelona again finished second, Venables lost his job – he was sacked in the September – but by October he had been installed as manager of Spurs. Under him they made steady progress, and by 1991 were celebrating an FA Cup triumph, while

Venables was being named as chief executive. Two years later, however, his contract as chief executive was terminated by fellow-directors, and so began the saga of strife, as the Venables-Sugar feud smouldered and then erupted. By 1994 Venables was being installed as England's team coach and – amid all the off-field problems which beset him – he was facing up to the demand for succeess in the 1996 European championships.

As he prepared his England team for a game against Portugal, Venables revealed that his legal costs were heading for £1 million, as he carried on the fight to clear his name over allegations being made about him off the field of play; and while the Football Association continued to try to make peace between the England coach and Sugar, Venables remained defiant as he said: 'I know I am battling on two fronts – on the pitch and in the courts. But you can't live your life looking over your shoulder ... financially, I am a seven-figure sum down in legal costs, and I know I could still get thrashed. But so much has been said and written about my football life and business career that I can't let it go unchallenged. I have to get something back in return. I need to keep fighting, and I will keep fighting'.

After one court appearance, Venables emerged to say: 'I am disappointed at the result. However, I feel significantly vindicated in that the claim was almost halved.' The county-court judge had given it as his opinion that some of the evidence from Venables, on oath, had been 'rather wanton' and not 'entirely reliable, to put it at its most charitable'. But Graham Kelly maintained: 'Terry retains our full support'. Sir Bert Millichip declared: 'Something incredibly outlandish and extremely serious would have to come out of the woodwork to make us change our minds' – and it was confirmed some days later that Venables had met FA officials for informal talks on a new contract. Yet Noel White, one of the men responsible for Venables' appointment in 1994, was saying: 'There are certain matters we must consider – when we come to discuss the renewal of his contract'.

Venables himself claimed it was 'in the best interests of the FA to get this matter resolved sooner, rather than later, well in advance of the (European) tournament. It would not be good for people at the FA if, come the end of the championship, they decided they didn't want to keep me. They would be left scurrying around to try to find a new man with only a few weeks to go before qualifying for the World Cup begins. Everyone involved must take a mature attitude and sort things out correctly'. Graham Kelly declared: 'The bottom line is that we must have a coach in place in August, even July, for the World Cup. We need to know what the situation is going to be, post-Euro '96.

Kelly admitted the Football Association was 'pinning an awful lot on the work of a mediator who had been appointed to try to resolve the Venables-Sugar feud. While Sugar had a libel action pending, Venables had a claim for wrongful dismissal as chief executive af Spurs, and Kelly conceded: 'High-profile disputes inevitably cast a shadow over the game'. The claims by Sugar and Venables were not due to be heard until after the European championship – which meant, of course, just at the time England would be embarking upon their World Cup venture for 1998. At one stage Sir Bert Millichip had taken the astonishing course of publicly calling for Venables and Sugar to quit feuding, in the best interests of the game. Sugar, indeed, had barred Venables from going to games at Tottenham where, as often as not, internationals and potential internationals would be on view. That ban was eventually lifted. Millichip's intervention came as he declared: 'For football's sake, the time has come to say enough is enough'. His plea had been in a letter which was delivered simultaneously to both Sugar and Venables.

Millichip wrote: 'Over the past two years, I have observed, with increasing sadness and frustration, your continuing feud. Its origins are well-documented. The depth of its bitterness is all too apparent. The publicity it continues to generate must be an irritation and often an embarrassment to both of you. It is, of course, a private matter, but because of the high profile of the game we serve it is a public matter, too. Those who thrive on denigrating football have unquestionably found a source of energy in your problems. The game itself can be the only definite loser, if this continues'. Millichip urged both men to meet and to make concessions.

On the football front, as Venables prepared his team for another friendly, this time against Switzerland, he referred to a county-court case in which he was involved as he said: 'Every time England have a game, something like this crops up. This court case will not stop me doing my job'. He insisted he was the victim of a witch-hunt. Meanwhile, an unnamed member of the Football Association's international committee was quoted as having expressed 'disquiet' and admitting: 'It's one thing after another … there always seems to be something else coming up. It does worry us – there's no getting away from it'.

The unnamed source claimed that 'unofficially, the situation gets discussed between the comittee, but it hasn't been talked about officially yet'. One sportswriter questioned if the Football Association had made the right choice in naming Venables as their man … 'the standard-bearer of the game'. He wrote: 'No-one has found Venables guilty of anything, but they worry at what is coming next'. The writer's verdict: 'The FA need to announce their position unequivocally, because football is not meant to be one long courtroom battle. The England job deserves and demands better'. The writer also reflected: 'The major problem the FA face, and one which is leading to increasing disquiet in the corridors of power, is how many cases there will be before the coach can concentrate without distraction on the task for which he was appointed – leading the country to a distinctive performance in the 1996 European championships'.

As if on cue, the Football Association made it plain that it was giving the England coach its full support. David Davies, the association's director of public affairs, declared:

'Terry Venables does not need votes of confidence … we all know how they are interpreted in football. The fact is that in January,1994, he was seen as unquestionably the best person to coach England to success in the European championship next summer. Despite all attempts to undermine him by unproven, sometimes wild and sometimes anonymous allegations, that remains the FA view 22 months later'. Noel White confirmed that 'our first priority has always been to give England the best possible chance of winning next year's European-championship finals. Terry Venables was our choice as the man to lead our effort … he remains that choice today. Those who seek to undermine him should be in no doubt of what they are in danger of doing. That is to undermine the prospects of our national team. The time has surely come for Terry Venables to be allowed to get on with the job he is performing on behalf of us all'.

Sir Bobby Charlton, who had criticised Venables' predecessor, Graham Taylor, voiced his fears about Euro '96 as he said he hoped Venables would be able to concentrate on football. 'It would be terrible if something cropped up a couple of months before the championship and the FA had to take him away from the job'. Sir Bobby maintained: 'He was the best man available at the time of his appointment'.

On the last day of November, 1995, it was reported that Venables was 'facing a near crisis as government investigators sought to disqualify him as a company director. The Department of Trade and industry has started proceedings against the England coach, following allegations of improper conduct of a company. DTI inspectors are pressing for the former Spurs manager and chief executive to be barred from running a private company for up to 15 years'. The DTI had not detailed the allegations, but it had pointed out that no criminal charges would be brought against Venables. It was said that the proceedings followed an 18-month-long investigation into the business affairs of four companies, and Venables' solicitor, confirming receipt of the DTI letter, commented: 'It's ironic that after two and a half years of allegations and inquiries, the only thing they have come up with is disqualification as a director'. The solicitor stressed that the DTI had found no grounds for criminal proceedings, while an FA spokesman said: 'We are fully aware of this development. Terry Venables is employed as coach to the England football team, and will continue to be so'. Venables' verdict: 'I am not guilty, and will fight this as I have fought all the other allegations that have been made against me'.

Then came a story concerning a VAT bill for £160,000 which had to be paid concerning Venables' Kensington club, Scribes West, and Ian Stott declared that 'it is Terry's financial management which is in question. No-one is helped by accusations of this nature, whether criminal or otherwise. This bears out what we did, in the sense that it was quite deliberate to make him coach, and not manager'. Stott confirmed: 'I was instrumental in that decision, and it has proved wise. Any administration or management as such is no part of his brief. It's not a question of not trusting him'.

When Venables travelled with Graham Kelly to Cheshire for a meeting with managers of clubs which had foundered in Europe during season 1995-96 (this was just before the draw for the third round of the FA Cup), he seemed to be his usual, chirpy self as it was confirmed yet again that the Football Association was still doing its utmost to achieve a settlement of the feud between the England coach and Alan Sugar. And while Noel White renewed the association's pledge that Venables remained their man for the England coaching job, Kelly came out with even stronger stuff.

He revealed that he and Sir Bert Millichip planned to discuss a new contract with the England coach. According to Kelly, 'we are going to be talking to Terry about his future, and what his feelings are – and soon. We will be exploring various avenues and, at this stage, the discussions would be restricted to myself, the chairman and Terry'. One observer pointed out that Ian Stott had 'stoked up the debate about the coach's future' and that White had defended Venables ... 'but it is significant that Kelly, the FA's most powerful figure, has made his position clear – that unless anything of a grave nature is proven, Venables remains the man to lead England'. And this, it was said, concerned not only the European championships, but a deal 'which would keep him as England coach until the 1998 World Cup finals'.

Kelly declared: 'Like the chairman, it is my wish that Terry will be able to carry on after the European championship when his current contract expires and through to the next World Cup. I certainly hope we are in that position and that circumstances allow us to do that'. There was a tail-end sentence, however, which suggested that all was not cut and dried. Kelly admitted: 'Obviously, the desire to offer Terry another contract presupposes a number of things'. Kelly did offer a hint of the way the Football Association's members were thinking when he said: 'At the moment, I don't know whether we will tie up a new deal by the summer, but on that front I recognize there are aspirations on both sides'. For his part, Venables said: 'It's good to hear that what was planned between us remains the same'. Kelly pointed out that the whole situation would be improved if the rift between Venables and Sugar could be healed – 'a lot of the problems are a direct or indirect result of Terry's fall-out with Alan Sugar ... we've made repeated attempts to resolve the matter, and will continue to do so'. To which Venables' reply was: 'I'm happy to hear that'. Sugar wasn't quoted.

By the beginning of 1996, it was reported that Venables 'faces a bitter battle with the FA international committee to get his new contract as England coach approved', and that 'a decision to reappoint him now will provoke an angry response from the committee, who are planning to block any attempt to rush it through'.

There was a reminder that 'key members Noel White and Ian Stott have already expressed reservations about offering Venables a new contract beyond the European championship before next summer's tournament begins ... they are concerned about the number of damaging court actions Venables is fighting, and how that could affect preparations for the World Cup qualifying matches, and the fact that there has been little discussion with them by Kelly or Sir Bert Millichip'. It was claimed that the 14-man international committee had planned to discuss Venables' future at the end of January, 1996 – 'but if the England coach's contract is settled before that date, the committee plans to call an emergency meeting to try to halt the process and have safeguards built in, relating to the team's performance in Euro '96, as well as the ramifications of all his legal actions'.

The first day of the New Year had brought the claim that Graham Kelly had placed 'the biggest question mark yet over the future of Terry Venables when he revealed that the FA's priority is a World Cup campaign with no distractions'. By mid-January, 1996, the die had been cast; Terry Venables had told the Football Association that he would be bowing out after the European championships – and the finger was being pointed at Noel White, chairman of the international committee, after a meeting with Venables, Kelly and Millichip in the Hyatt Regency hotel in Birmingham on the morning of Sunday, December 17, 1995. It was there that matters came to a head, and one newspaper depicted the scene with an artist's impression of what was termed the showdown. Venables was portrayed wagging a finger at White as he leaned forward, with Millichip and Kelly, looking suitably pensive, in the background. On the morning of Sunday, January 15, 1996, two national newspapers went into detail about the December 17 meeting.

In the *News of the World*, Venables claimed that when he met White he asked if he had the backing of the Football Association – but White's failure to deliver a vote of confidence forced him to make his shock decision to quit. *The Mail on Sunday* had White 'shifting nervously in his chair' … this 'grey and relatively anonymous figure was not relishing the prospect of the meeting', while Venables 'was in no mood for niceties'.

It was reported that 'an angry Venables waited for a response' to his question and that White 'gritted his teeth, stood his ground and muttered that, unfortunately, he was unable to provide such an assurance'. Whatever the minute details of the matter, when it came down to that fateful meeting, on the day the stories appeared in the two Sunday papers, I talked at some length to a source close to the powers that be at Lancaster Gate – and if Noel White, seemingly, was being subjected to the flak, it was made clear to me that several of his fellow-members of the Football Association were against extending Terry Venables' contract. My source told me: 'I, for one, had reservations from the start, but you back your committee. When Terry was given the job in the first place, he was given it only until the European championships – there was no question then of looking at the situation again at the start of 1996. It was going to be left until after the European championships'.

My source confirmed what the *Mail on Sunday* had said – that Venables had given an undertaking to try to dispose of his Kensington club, Scribes. 'That was a condition on which he was given the job, although there were other things which I am not prepared to talk about. But the fact is that in January, 1996, he still hadn't sold Scribes'. My source claimed that 'there were things we didn't know that have cropped up...' this was in reply to something the England coach had said on television only a few days previously, when being interviewed by Bob Wilson. The former Arsenal goalkeeper had surprised me, and others, by the manner in which he appeared to be treating the resignation of Venables – almost as important, one might think, as the Second Coming. One writer claimed Wilson had 'grovelled', that he had been 'ingratiating' as he had talked to Venables. The England coach declared that the Football Association had been aware of the situation regarding himself from day one – but, as my source said, 'there were things we didn't know that have cropped up'. My informant maintained that Venables 'pushed in October and November for an extension to his contract, and we resisted that one ... and at the end of the day he has switched it around as if he didn't want an extension'. Graham Kelly was said to have revealed that the Football Association 'moved heaven and earth' to keep Venables; my source said Kelly would have been going beyond his remit to offer the coach a new deal – 'it's the committee's job to offer an extension of contract'.

In fact, according to my source, the sub-committee would be required to put the matter to the full international committee, for final approval. When I put the question, 'Was Terry Venables trying to push the Football Association into giving him a new contract?' the answer came back bluntly, and in a word: 'Absolutely'. And when I repeated the query as to whether or not the international committee knew all about the situation regarding the England coach 'from day one', I was told: 'Not true'. Venables, you will recall, had claimed that 'some people with small minds are making assumptions – they believe I am trying to steamroller through a new contract. That is not the case'. So it seemed as if he and at least one of his employers would have to agree to differ, when it came to interpreting attitudes. Ian Stott had said it was 'a key issue' as to whether or not one man or the whole committee could agree a contract ... Kelly himself admitted that 'a number of issues that have come to light in the two years since we appointed Terry have been greater than we might have expected at the time. There's no point in being dishonest about that'. Stott maintained that he was 'seeking to establish the procedure by which he (Venables) is given an extension to his contract – or whether it is rejected'.

The England coach was pictured – with a newspaper reporter by his side – leaving his Kensington club after what was termed 'a day of turmoil for English football', and, at the age of 53, Venables clearly had experienced just about everything that football had to offer. Now after having made public his decision to turn his back on the England coaching job, once the European championships had come and gone, he would be in a position to turn his attention to the court cases he was seeking to win. Venables, indeed, knew all about what he had once termed the power and the glory in the game ... he had declared that it was managers such as Alex Ferguson and Kenny Dalglish who could bask in the glory – but that it was men like Martin Edwards and Jack Walker who wielded the real power. When Liverpool met Leeds United at Anfield in January, 1996, there was an intriguing comment on the appearance of the England coach and his boss at the Football Association ... it was reported that Venables 'resisted the chance to put on a public display of unity with his estranged FA boss, Noel White ... he remained seated five rows behind Liverpool director White, his main Lancaster Gate protagonist'.

Football, of course, is an emotive game; one in which every fan feels entitled to have his or her say. For instance, Kate Hoey, MP, who follows the fortunes of Arsenal. When I contacted her about the speeches she had made in Parliament on the subject of football, she cleared up one point for me – about her role at one time as 'an adviser to Arsenal'. She told me: 'Before becoming an MP, I worked first for Arsenal, later for Spurs, Chelsea and Brentford as an educational adviser for their trainees – advising them off the field, such as on completing academic qualifications and arranging courses, the importance of planning for their careers after football, and giving them some tips on how to give a successful interview etc.' She also said: 'I have never been employed to give advice on team selection or tactics (although, as with every fan, I always had a view), nor to give any lofty advice about any club's business activities or public profile'. One noted newspaper columnist expressed the view that in the event of Tony Blair coming to power, he could do a lot worse than make Ms. Hoey the Minister for Sport.

Going back to Terry Venables, who had been one of the subjects of Ms. Hoey's attentions in the House of Commons, he, too, looked to the future after Euro '96, as he urged those who might be in line as his successor not to be afraid of the England job. 'It has been dubbed the impossible job, but I wouldn't agree with that. Maybe there are those who fear the consequences of taking charge of England, but I don't see that. Whatever you are in, you should aspire to the pinnacle of that profession ... in football, that has to be taking charge of the England side'.

One of his predecessors, Bobby Robson, had this to say about Terry Venables: 'He's a fine coach and a shrewd tactician, and England are going to need large chunks of both those attributes if we are to do well in the European championship; even with home advantage'. Another of Venables' predecessors, Graham Taylor, had been critical of the decision to accept a World Cup-qualifying programme which left England with their final fixture in Italy in November, 1997. Venables' answer: 'Graham is entitled to his opinion. Even if we'd managed to have our ideal choice, someone would have criticised us. What we were more concerned about was the game before Italy, which is Moldova at home. Had we finished with Italy at home, there would have been three away games in succession before that, which wouldn't have been good for us'.

As for Euro '96, Venables was still 'in upbeat mood' after a training session at Bisham Abbey. 'The seeds of our preparation have been sown. I'm delighted with what we have achieved'. After two practice games and watching videos of how the players had performed, Venables was saying, also: 'I've had a lot of feed-back. They asked the right questions, and we're getting somewhere. We've had to cram a lot in … they've shown how well they can handle the information coming in. They are up for what we're about. I've always believed that the higher you go, the more you have to take in. It you're going to be world-class, you have to open your mind'. Venables responded positively, too, to criticism of a pre-tournament tour to the Far East – he believed his squad would be able to make full use of the trip by being together, as well as by preparing for the real thing.

He had been in similar mood after what was termed 'the slender victory over lethargic Bulgaria' – the point being made was that 'his record in his initial 14 games in charge of England is inferior to any of the previous six managers'. The Venables view: 'I'm sure I'll be where I want to be by the time of the first game'. That was scheduled for June 8, 1996, against Switzerland. Venables again: 'I've learned that it's no good saying one established system of play will be enough. I'm trying to establish what the players can and cannot do. It may require them to be comfortable with different types of systems even in the same game, if we are to achieve our objectives. It is of vital importance to establish a nucleus who will be confident when they pull on the England shirt. The intention is to establish a team plan that won't only look good, but will provide a winning formation'. By that time, there were two games left – against Croatia and Hungary – for England to flex their muscles on home soil.

The England coach didn't duck the issue as he declared: 'The onus is on me now … I believe we have got the right players, and it is my responsibility to set the game plan to suit us and to get the players to do what I want. But always, most important of all, it is up to me to get it right so that the players produce on the day'. Early in March, 1996, he had reason to celebrate what, as one writer said, 'he hopes will be the first of a sequence of victories both on and off the pitch this year'. This particular victory was in the High Court, as he was awarded £50,000, plus £100,000 costs, in a judgment against Paul Kirby, a former business partner who was also an FA councillor.

Venables said the court victory had boosted his morale and could not have come at a better time. 'It has always been my priority to get the England side in the right shape for the championship … I've tried to keep other things separate, but it can only help if something positive happens, like this. It's a nice feeling to see some of the things I've been saying all along vindicated in courts.' Yet he admitted, also, that 'all those other court cases are still there, so my position has not altered. But after having so many knocks in the past, it's nice to feel that things might be beginning to go my way. Hopefully, that will be the case with the England team this summer'. Legal representatives for Kirby, the FA's New Zealand representative who sat on two influential committees at Lancaster Gate, claimed the costs ruling meant he would be out of pocket, and in a statement Kirby said he would be appealing. In the meantime, it was football business as usual for Terry Venables, since various court appearances in which he was due to be involved had been held over until after the European championship.

As the debate over Venables' future in football continued, Sir Bobby Charlton declared: 'I think every effort should be made to keep Terry ... with him in charge, we can win the World Cup. We have started to play the passing game again and it's been translated into the England team. I think we are capable of doing well. To change now would be a retrograde step'. Twenty-four hours later, however, it was being reported that 'Graham Kelly insisted that the Football Association will not be tempted to try to persuade Venables to reconsider his decision to quit as England coach'. And this 'despite a growing clamour for the FA to abandon their search for a successor and ask Venables to change his mind and stay on for another two years'. Kelly was quoted: 'I am well aware of what people have been suggesting, but it is not something we will consider. The idea of seeking to ask Terry to reconsider is not on the agenda of the sub-committee. The last thing we want now is any more uncertainty – it is now for us to find a new man'. And while Venables himself was ready to hand over to a successor a World Cup dossier, he made it clear that whoever came in, 'it is not possible for me to integrate the next England manager into my European-championship preparations'. The World Cup was 'completely separate' from Euro '96, and 'I'm sure the new manager would understand that ... I do not want anything to disrupt my preparations for the European championship'.

By mid-April, with the European championships just eight weeks and one day distant, there were further words – which could be interpreted as good news and bad news. The bad news first... 'Terry Venables has been told the BBC will not back down over Panorama allegations of misconduct in his business dealings, despite his claims that documents used to back up the claims were not authentic. The England coach is suing the BBC over the accusations, and has demanded an investigation into the validity of the evidence produced in two programmes, which were made by Martin Bashir in 1993 and 1994' . Bashir, of course, was the man who famously interviewed Princess Diana on television. The BBC responded to Venables by issuing a statement: 'We stand by the authenticity of the documents referred to in the Panorama programme'. Venables repeated his earlier assertions that he would fight to clear his name – 'I would rather have been stabbed in the heart than put up with some of the stuff that has been thrown at me', was his somewhat dramatic riposte.

The good news? – That came for the Football Association, after earlier gloomy predictions that Euro '96 would turn out to be less than a money-spinner. On the day the Venables story about the BBC broke, it was also reported that 'soaring interest' in the summer championships meant that the tournament 'is heading to become a

£150 million bonanza'. A rush for tickets had contributed £50 million towards this projected figure, virtually making sure that 95 per cent of the seats would be filled (15 of the 31 games had already been sold out, and the competition organizers were forecasting at least 10 more full houses). Fees from television would inject another £50 million into the kitty, and a similar amount would come from commercial spin-offs. Tournament-director Glen Kirton said: 'I expect we will sell out most of the games... I think we've got it just about right'. He was referring to the pricing of tickets with that last remark. The interest, it was said, demonstrated 'just how big the European championship is ... we could even be looking at a complete sell-out'. So far, so good; all that was required now was for Terry Venables and his team to put the icing on the cake by showing that they could emerge as top dogs, at the end of this prestigious tournament. Which, of course, would be easier said than done – as had been pointed out, seven of the teams in the last eight of the 1994 World Cup had come from Europe. And, of course, England had not been among them.

Terry Venables discusses tactics with Peter Beardsley at an England training session.

CHAPTER 15

ON APRIL 20, 1996 – the anniversary of Hitler's birthday – Terry Venables dismissed renewed speculation that he could be talked into staying on as England coach after Euro '96. Five days later, Bryan Robson ruled himself out of the running for the job when he agreed to remain as Middlesbrough's manager until 1999. Venables: 'There is still a combination of reasons why I have decided to go, and major court cases to be resolved … for those reasons, the situation cannot change'. A projected meeting between Venables and the Football Association's chief executive, Graham Kelly, was not aimed at trying to persuade Venables to stay – according to David Davies, the FA's public-affairs spokesman, the meeting would be 'to talk about the succession'. As for Robson, the 39-year-old former England captain – 'once considered the natural heir to Venables' – he was saying: 'I like the everyday involvement… I think the England job, if it were offered, would have come a bit too early. I'd like to have more experience at club level before I took that step. I still have a lot to learn from management. Being involved with Terry has given me a great insight into what the job means, and I'll be better equipped for it, if it comes my way in future'.

One of England's current players, Paul Gascoigne, had come out strongly three days previously and 'challenged the Football Association to persuade Venables to stay on and complete the transformation of our international fortunes'. Gazza: 'The public are with him, the players are with him'. And he added: 'It will be a tragedy for English football if we don't snap him up again – because someone else will'.

Tragedy or not, the guessing game was in full flow again… 'Glenn Hoddle emerged last night as favourite to be the new England manager' – this was in mid-April, 1996 – just three months after a story which ran: 'Gerry Francis and Glenn Hoddle yesterday joined the queue of managers discounting any interest in succeeding Terry Venables as England coach. Francis and Hoddle reduced the Football Association's options by following the example of Kevin Keegan and Ray Wilkins'. Francis was quoted: 'Although my agreement with Tottenham expires this summer, at present I am of the same opinion as I was two years ago when I was interviewed about the England position: if my future is in football, it would be at club level'. And Hoddle: 'I should imagine the FA want continuity, and that's why Bryan Robson would be my choice'. Like Francis, Hoddle would be available because his contract with Chelsea was due to run out at the end of season 1995-96.

By mid-April, it was rumoured that Chelsea's 38-year-old team boss had been 'informally' interviewed by members of the sub-committee dealing with the appointment of a successor to Venables. Hoddle himself was still talking about negotiating a new deal with Chelsea, though he was said to have become 'increasingly disillusioned' at the inability of the club to get down to the nitty-gritty – 'No-one has told me what money might be available, and I need to know exactly how the club will be run. I've made my feelings clear to the board'. Meanwhile, Jimmy Armfield, special adviser to the FA's sub-committee, reiterated: 'We want someone in place before Euro '96'. And while Hoddle had his supporters, so did Francis – one sportswriter pointed out that this was 'one man who stands out from the crowd'. He had captained England at 23 and, as a manager, 'his record of manufacturing silk purses out of sows' ears throughout the leagues is near enough incomparable in the modern game'. It was pointed out that, of other possibles, Joe Royle still had a sizeable task on his hands at Everton, that Kevin Keegan's contract still had seven years to run. Early in the game, Keegan had said: 'I am interested in managing nobody but Newcastle'. And Wilkins? – The man who won 84 caps and was quoted at 20-1 in the England betting, said: 'I don't think I even come into contention'. By January, 1995, the betting odds showed that Gerry Francis was rated at 5-2, Keegan had drifted out to 11-10, Bryan Robson was 6-4, Howard Wilkinson 10-1, and Hoddle and Joe Royle were quoted at 16-1. Clearly, when it came to naming Venables' successor, it was a real guessing game.

Jimmy Armfield had stressed one point – that 'the strategy has not changed'; by which he meant the overall structure on the coaching side, where Venables had originally brought in Robson to work with the senior squad, with Wilkins operating alongside Dave Sexton at Under-21 level. 'The plan was for Bryan and Ray to be taught the ways of coaching and management in international football. That was the point of the structure. Terry has announced that he wants to move on, but the coaching set-up we have is as good as I believe we can get at present'. Armfield did add: 'But it's not for me to attempt to name the new man'. And when the new man did arrive, he picked his own men.

Two other names figured on the media's list of possibles – Nottingham Forest boss Frank Clark, who was known to be highly rated in the top echelons of the game, and Howard Wilkinson, who in eight years had taken Leeds out of the Second Division and to the pinnacle of the Premiership, with a Wembley final thrown in. Wilkinson, however, had seen the second half of season 1995-96 bring him little but trouble, as Leeds supporters turned upon him and results went awry. Yet, like Clark, he was highly rated at Lancaster Gate. Indeed, one story declared that he was wanted to occupy the dual roles of England coach and technical director … he was viewed from within Lancaster Gate 'as the sole candidate to mastermind both important tasks'. At 52, Wilkinson had just about seen and done it all, and he was the FA's 'primary target'. Should he or Leeds United prove intractable, however, Clark would become the next target. 'There has been plenty of talk inside Lancaster Gate about the high calibre of Clark, both as a coach and as a man', an FA 'insider' was said to have revealed.

Wilkinson, 14 years a manager, is not the most charismatic character in the game – 'I cannot help the face God has given me', he said. 'People just look at my expression and categorise me as a bit of a miserable sod. They don't make the slightest attempt to get to know me. But that is the nature of the business'. It was said that if people were prepared to peer behind the mask of inscrutability, they would discover 'a jaunty character with a passion for top-class claret and havana cigars, as well as a taste in shirts and suits to rival the flamboyance of Ron Atkinson'. Oh, yes… 'and a profound philosophy'. As Wilkinson spoke about the worry of managing at club level, he asked this question: 'Can the excitement of the job overcome the pressure, especially if we are talking about England?' At that time, he still managed Leeds…

In the final analysis, Glenn Hoddle evidently thought so, because after spending more than four hours locked in talks with Matthew Harding at Chelsea, he gave the Football Association the answer it wanted to hear … he would become the successor to Terry Venables. He was paraded at a Press conference on the afternoon of Thursday, May 2, 1996, and was said to be accepting a four-year deal worth around £1 million. At 38, he was the youngest-ever team boss of England. Hoddle, born on October 27, 1957, at Hayes, in Middlesex, had shown that he could be loyal as a player – having become a Tottenham Hotspur apprentice in 1974 and signed professional forms the following year, he remained at Spurs until 1987, totalling 494 appearances and scoring 100 goals. He made his debut at the age of 18, as a substitute in a game against Norwich City, scored against Stoke City on his full debut in 1976, and scored at Wembley in 1979 as he made his bow for England, against Bulgaria.

In 1981, he was claiming an FA Cup-winners medal in the final against Manchester City, and a year later won a runners-up medal in the League Cup final against Liverpool. He scored in both FA Cup finals against Queen's Park Rangers to claim his second winner's medal in a row, after the replay, and figured in the Spurs side which lost to Coventry in the 1987 final. Then it was off to Monaco, as Spurs did a £750,000 deal, and Hoddle earned a championship medal with the French club. By 1988 he was bowing out as an England player, with 53 caps to his credit, and by 1990 seemingly hanging up his boots because of injury problems. However, by 1991 he was making a comeback as a non-contract player, and when he became player-manager of Swindon, he totalled 75 appearances and scored three goals. In 1993 he was scoring the first goal as Swindon beat Leicester City in a Premiership promotion play-off, but a month later he was on his way to Chelsea as player-manager. He scored one goal in his 48 games before becoming manager in 1995, and finally, after having revealed to his players that the England job was his – if he wanted it – he decided to leave Stamford Bridge and chance his arm in the international arena. It was said to be 'the biggest decision of Hoddle's career … stay in club football and try to build Chelsea into a force rivalling Manchester United and Newcastle, or lead his country towards the

1998 World Cup.'

As Hoddle looked ahead to his first match in charge – the qualifier against Moldova on September 1, 1996 ... just nine weeks after the final of the European championships – former England hero Gary Lineker was giving a warm welcome and a vote of confidence. But the warning signals had already been hoisted, hours before Hoddle had finally said yes to the job ... the chief football writer of the *Daily Mirror*, Harry Harris, offered the view that while Hoddle could expect to be praised, should he succeed, the price of failure would be the fate which had befallen Graham Taylor, to name but one. He could expect to be hammered by the media if it all went wrong. Hoddle, who admitted that managing England had been 'a burning ambition from a very young age', said: 'If I were worried about the media pressure, I wouldn't have taken the job'. He added: 'That is not a good reason to turn the job down, any way.'

By one of those twists of fate, Hoddle took the job on the very day that Peter Swales, former chairman of the international committee, died. For it was on May 2 that Swales, victim of two heart attacks which had put him in hospital, died suddenly. This was the man who had talked to me, only a matter of weeks previously, about the effects of media pressure on the various international team bosses, and as Swales's career was recorded – just like Hoddle's – on television, the man he appointed for a brief spell as general manager of Manchester City was also pictured, talking about the time Swales himself called it quits at Maine Road. John Maddock, once a newspaper colleague of mine, had this to say about Swales: 'He had had enough of the vicious hate campaign... I think the final straw came when his mother, who was 87 years old, was threatened.' Those words, surely, provide a great deal of food for thought about the way the game has gone. Food for thought especially, perhaps, for someone who was about to take over what Peter Swales had called 'the hardest job in football.'

CHAPTER 16

ON Monday, May 27, 1996, one headline proclaimed: England a Joke Before the Off. Another said: Hong Kong Horror. Terry Venables' players had just managed to scrape a 1-0 victory over an assorted eleven described as 'a motley crew of has-beens and never-weres', and former England player Trevor Francis, commentating for satellite television, termed this the worst England display he had ever seen. It was recorded: 'A couple of the players were too ashamed to even touch the cup awarded…' Thus ended the pre-Euro '96 trip to China (a 3-0 victory there) and Hong Kong. There were fewer than 14 days to go to the start of the real thing.

That same evening, on Channel 4 television back home, former England managers were grilled by Greg Dyke about the media … in turn, Alf Ramsey, (speaking at the tine of the 1970 World Cup), Bobby Robson and Graham Taylor had their say. Robson, arriving at Heathrow airport from Portugal, was met by Dyke, who mentioned that had he still been England manager, there would have been a posse of Pressmen waiting to besiege him. As it was, Dyke had no opposition. Robson, then managing FC Porto, had shed that grey, haunted look he so often carried when in charge of England; he looked fit and tanned, years younger and very relaxed. He maintained that he had no regrets about having taken the England job, and he would recommend it to other candidates … even though 'if it goes wrong, it will partly destroy you.'

There was a flashback to the 1970 era, with Ramsey declaring: 'I am treated with rudeness… I don't think there has been a word invented that would describe the mannerisms of some of the people I have been confronted with'. And Dyke talked of a love-hate relationship between the England manager and the tabloids over the last 30 years'. It was the tabloids who were blamed 'for seeing off most of the England managers'. Ramsey's reaction, back in 1970, to some of the media interrogators? – 'They stick their faces in front of me…'

Robson referred to the time he was called a 'plonker', Taylor talked about the headline which said 'Swedes 2, Turnips 1' – he smiled as he said he reckoned it was a good headline, though he also said he believed his family had been hurt by the description. Another headline, referring to Robson, declared that England Mustafa New Boss (this was after a match in the Middle East), and Robson spoke of his feeling of disbelief when he realised that one reporter aboard the England aircraft had said: 'I'm here to fry Bobby Robson'. Robson declared: 'That's beyond the bounds of decency.' Going back to the Turnips headline, Taylor – whose father had long been in journalism – was frank enough to say: 'It's not as if I am not aware of what certain sections of the Press would be looking for.' Even so, as an only son, 'I am sure my parents were hurt.'

Greg Dyke didn't talk only to the former England managers; he talked to the men who write for the papers … notably Harry Harris, of the *Daily Mirror,* and former *Sun* sports editor Brian Alexander, who claimed that the 'Turnips' headline 'was supposedly a bit of fun' – though he did admit: 'It was interpreted as being vicious.' Alexander also conceded that repeated references to the 'Turnip' had been over the top – indeed, he repented over the headline, though inferring also that while 'I wouldn't do it now', 'if I were sports editor of the *Sun,* clinging to my job…' When it came to a headline in the *Mirror* about 'A Norse' around the neck of Terry Venables (he was pictured in a noose), Alexander said this was 'not acceptable'.

Bobby Robson claimed that sports editors must come in for some criticism. He also spoke of a circulation war and said that England were expected to be winners every time out. But 'there are no easy matches in world football any more.'

Graham Taylor backed this assertion by pointing out that England had won the World Cup once and reached the semi-finals, but that they had also failed to qualify on more than one occasion – including 1994 (when he was manager). His conclusion: 'So we are not very good … our record at international level is nothing to shout about. It never has been.' And there was this: 'You are in a no-win situation a lot of the time … the England manager's job can be very difficult. If you take the England job at around the age of 38 or 40, you are probably putting 15 years of your career at risk'. What he meant was that should you fail (as he was adjudged to have done), then you carried what he termed 'the baggage' of that perceived failure with you.

Bobby Robson declared that 'if you take the job and you don't win, they (the media) go for you.' And he further declared that young managers with families could hardly be blamed for shying away from such a situation. Graham Taylor believed the people who did the criticising 'don't have a real understanding of the people they hurt, sometimes', and that after so long 'you draw a line and say enough is enough.'

According to Greg Dyke, the *Mirror* had headed a campaign against Terry Venables, and Harry Harris had been Venables' 'tormentor in chief.' Harris himself admitted: 'I can see why managers don't want to take the job where their private lives are turned upside down.' But 'it goes with the territory', and 'I am doing my job.' When Dyke produced an England manager's blazer and suggested that Harris might just fancy trying it on for size, the reporter smiled, shook his head and acknowledged the truth of Dyke's statement that 'it isn't for you'.

And so the programme switched to the Press conference which announced the appointment of Glenn Hoddle in succession to Terry Venables. Harris was in the audience and so was Dyke, while Hoddle was flanked by Venables and Graham Kelly, chief executive of the Football association. Dyke stood, to launch a loaded question: 'You were quoted in 1994 as saying the only thing that worried you about taking the England job would be the media, and the effect it would have on your family. Does it still worry you?'

Hoddle: 'If I had worried about that, I wouldn't have taken the job... I am sure Terry can give me a few pointers on it.'

And as Venables sat, smiling knowingly, Hoddle added: 'That (media pressure) wouldn't be a reason for turning this job down.' Cue for Venables to say: 'He's well qualified to deal with that.' Back to Harry Harris who, when quizzed by Dyke about Hoddle's appointment, smiled also as he said: 'Right man for the job... I think he will win over the media, and they should give him a turnip-free first year.' Which left Dyke to sum up: 'So, in a year's time we can be here all over again, with Glenn Hoddle under siege.' Or words to that effect. The title of the Channel 4 programme, by the way, was *Fair Game*. As for Hoddle, it wasn't the next England team boss who was to come under siege, but the players themselves after a storm had broken about their ears. A media storm, that is.

Hard on the heels of the criticisms concerning the on-field display in Hong Kong came a welter of words about a trip to a night club by some of the players, after the game. It was reported: 'England players went on a binge days before next week's Euro '96 championships, it emerged last night.' Some it was said, 'knocked back beer and cocktails in Hong Kong's China Jump night club. "They drank a lot," said the manager.' More followed... 'The players drank on the homeward flight, when £5,000 damage was caused to the plane.' And what happened on flight CX251, the Cathay Pacific 747, caused a war of words.

There were newspaper pictures of some of the England players in the Hong Kong night club – one front-page shot featured a player with his shirt 'almost ripped in two by boisterous team-mates', while other players were also pictured on the back page and elsewhere as it was reported that, with Paul Gascoigne's 29th birthday on the agenda, 'some members of the England squad let their hair down.' Not only that; it was reported that some players had taken part in the 'dentist's-chair' experience, which involved having alcoholic refreshment poured down their throats. Then came the claims that during the flight back, £5,000 worth of damage had been done, involving two personal TV's and a table. All of which brought the wrath of the media – and the condemnation of a former England World Cup hero – down on the players' heads.

From Zurich, it was reported that Sir Bobby Charlton 'shook with emotion as he spoke of his horror and shame at the antics of some of the England squad on their return from their tour to the Far East', and the great man was quoted: 'This has made the whole of the country ashamed ... you just don't do it. It's terrible when I come to a place like this and somebody shows you these stories. You find it difficult to answer – it's embarrassing.' Charlton said that in his playing days such ill-discipline would not have been tolerated, and he would have been expected to be sent home in similar circumstances. A message echoed by his former England boss, Sir Alf Ramsey. The Charlton vedict: 'I would think somebody at the FA should do something, because these players were on England business, and you would expect them to have some answers as to why it happened.

'I'm not saying anybody should be thrown out of the championships ... that would be shooting yourself in the foot. Nevertheless, punishment could still be deferred. I think the people at the FA should take action when everything is clear. Quite simply, there are rules when you're on tour – you're representing your country, and if it gets out of hand, well...' And from FA chairman Sir Bert Millichip came a warning that the association would crack down heavily on any England players found guilty of drunken behaviour. He was quoted: 'If I discover that it was serious, then the punishment will be serious.' The FA's chief executive, Graham Kelly, had a word or two: 'Pictures of people at the height of a party rarely look appealing to outsiders in the cold light of day. These were certainly no exception.' The official stance was that coach Terry Venables must dig out the facts of the affair ... and he, it was reported, 'will read the riot act when his 22-strong squad report for Euro '96 duty tonight.'

Venables' reaction: 'I will hold an inquiry. If there are people to be punished, they will be punished. If the reports are accurate, the culprits will be severely dealt with. But I will not throw them to the wolves, just for the sake of it.' Venables, who had been on board the Cathay Pacific flight, along with FA officials – though not in the same section as the players – insisted that his 22 men would remain 'in position' for the European championships. Venables said he wanted his inquiry to be 'done and dusted' before training on the Monday morning.

A statement from him later said he had spent several hours talking to the players about the various allegations, and that three of them were 'very angry' that they had taken the blame publicly – 'and without justification, they believe' – for the reported damage on the aircraft. 'They told me they were seeking legal advice on compensation for the harm to their reputations.' Most of the squad seemed to have been 'totally unaware' of any problems on the flight until they had arrived home, and more than nine hours had passed after touchdown before Cathay Pacific had contacted the Football Association.

Then came the public conclusion: 'The England squad has accepted collective responsibility for what has happened. The matter is being dealt with internally. Financial penalties will be imposed. The players have expressed their sincere regret over the incident. This is the first time I have had any complaints about the behaviour of senior players while I have been in charge.' So, at last, it was admitted that there had been an 'incident', and it was reported that the FA had paid Cathay Pacific some £4,000 in compensation. One respected sportswriter, the *Daily Mail's* Neil Harman, claimed that the phrase 'collective responsibility' was 'just a euphemism for taking the easy way out ... don't name names, simply tar everyone with the same brush that should have been turned on the real culprits.'

Harman claimed that 'not for the first time, the FA have completely misread public opinion', and I have to say that of all the people (ordinary fans) with whom I discussed the matter, the vast majority expressed a single viewpoint: that the Football Association should have named the guilty party or parties, made it clear he or they would not play for England in the European championships, and stated publicly the punishment imposed. Then, no matter how well or poorly England might have performed in the championships, at least the nation as a whole could have held its head up high. As it was, people told me – and I found it impossible to disagree – that even should England win the tournament, the achievement would be tarnished by memories of what had gone before; not least the fact that, as one fan put it, 'what happened was brushed aside and hidden behind the curtain of collective responsibility.'

Of course, the media went overboard, in some cases – though it might, in the final analysis, find that some of its own fingers were going to be burned, as the discerning members of the public, not to mention politicians (naturally), voiced their disapproval of the treatment being meted out. One sportswriter of genuine standing, Ian Wooldridge, was prompted to comment upon the about-turn achieved by some of the papers as England progressed through the various rounds. And some of the tabloids who had screamed loudest in protest at the start were now shouting just as loudly in praise of the players they had savaged. Not that the papers were the only ones who could be criticised.

One leader column did express the view that 'the FA has done the impossible – it has made the dithering Ministry of Agriculture, Fisheries and Food look decisive.' The leader accused the Football Association of 'abdication' – and there would be many who would agree with that. As for the incident aboard the Cathay Pacific flight, Graham Kelly declared that he wasn't aware of any incident during or directly after the flight, 'which I find strange.' Fair enough. 'It wasn't until mid-afternoon on Tuesday that I first heard anything... I haven't spoken to Cathay Pacific directly, but they appear to be saying that two TV sets were broken...' Kelly spoke also about the players having been 'model professionals throughout the trip', but conceded that if the allegations were proved, the person concerned could expect to hear about it – 'we will have a very strong word with him, remind him of his responsibilities, and make him pay for the damage.'

Neil Harman reminded people that little more than a week previously one of the England players had been pleading publicly 'for England fans not to turn Euro '96 into a nightmare of hooliganism', and he claimed that police now wanted to interview several England players. Football Association spokesman Steve Double said: 'We accept that the damage was caused in the section where the England players sat.' However, it was also said that on the Far East tour, England's players had been 'exemplary ambassadors.' And so the debate raged as to who had done what, with talk of some players contemplating legal action against some of the more sensational tabloids.

Finally, of course, Euro '96 did get under way, with due pomp and ceremony, and we came to the football. Ah, yes the football…

It was England 1, Switzerland 1; England 2, Scotland 0; and England 4, Holland 1. So the group matches ended with the host nation on top and through to the quarter-finals, where they would meet Spain. England versus Switzerland? – It was generally accepted that England played poorly in the second half, that they were somewhat unfortunate to have a penalty awarded against them, but that, overall, the Swiss thoroughly deserved their draw. The media bullets were being fired after the first skirmish.

England versus Scotland? – It was generally accepted that Alan Shearer at last was making the kind of impact his scoring reputation deserved, and that Gascoigne's goal was a wondrous thing to behold. Having said that, at 1-0 for England, the match was in the balance as Scotland's captain, Gary McAllister, stepped up to take a penalty. David Seaman, who denied Gordon Durie a goal by making a brilliant save, also denied McAllister and his team-mates an equalizer, as he pulled off another magnificent save – but had that spot-kick gone home, who knows how the match would have ended? – It could certainly be argued that the Scots had shot themselves in the foot.

England versus Holland? – All that was needed was a draw, and both teams would be through to the quarter-finals. Strangely, after both contestants had announced their intention of going for victory, the Dutch seemed to take a very laid-back approach, and it proved to be their undoing. Shearer and Sheringham each scored twice as England produced probably their finest all-round display since the World Cup final in 1966, and the Dutch, in the end, were fortunate to finish 4-1 down and so scrape through to the quarter-finals.

By this time, some of the tabloids were doing a complete somersault – instead of vitriolic criticism, they were becoming jingoistic in the extreme, as they lauded the players they had so abused in print, and it seemed that all England needed to do was to turn up against Spain, in order to reach the semi-finals. Venables and his players must have pondered upon how swiftly things could change, even in a game where a period of 24 hours is a long time. Adios, Amigos! ran one headline … and that was before the match had been played. The more sober-minded of the scribes reflected upon what had actually happened, once England had won the battle with the 1996 Spanish Armada.

In short, the players representing Spain demonstrated for 120 minutes that, by and large, they had the measure of England, notably when it came to moving the ball around smoothly and creating problems in their opponents' 18-yard box. Indeed they got the ball into England's net twice before 90 minutes were up, claimed they should have had a penalty when Gascoigne committed a foul – and, for my money, one of the offside decisions given against the Spaniards was wrong, and a goal should have been allowed to stand. In that event, of course, England would not have been allowed the luxury of competing in a penalty shoot-out – though it has to be admitted that when it came to the spot-kick crunch. they found four heroes in Shearer, Platt, Pearce (especially Pearce) and Gascoigne. Spain's failure with two kicks – one of them brilliantly saved by Seaman – meant that England won 4-2, to go into a semi-final tie with Germany. Which prompted an outburst of near-hysteria from the more sensational tablolds.

In turn, this gave television the opportunity to publicise the fact that the Press Complaints Commission had been almost inundated with calls protesting about the newspapers' treatment of the England-Germany game. One headline fairly screamed Achtung! Surrender; and there were references to Fritz and inferences that England would win this war as they had won the one half a century earlier.

The *Mirror*, the *Sun* and the *Star* were all featured on TV as their front-page headlines were displayed on the eve of the match, and *Mirror* editor Piers Morgan attempted to pass off his paper's contribution as a bit of fun. The Germans who were interviewed clearly didn't see it that way, although they showed dignity and restraint in their own comments.

Dignity and restraint ... these themes were taken up by Terry Venables as he urged England supporters not to turn the semi-final confrontation into a war. 'I know how much it means to everyone but, at the end of the day (as the saying goes in Soccer), it is football, not war. I just hope the fans understand that. We want them behind us again, but I don't want to see them so whipped up that they spoil things. I want them to respect both national anthems and realise this is a football match. A huge game, yes – but still a football match.'

Venables again: 'I will remind my players that they must go into this game with cool heads – I don't want them to get carried away by outside influences. It disgusts me when I see pictures of some players published with tin hats being put on their heads. It is not just an insult to the Germans; it is an insult to the intelligence of the English people and those who have fought for their country in wars. Remember, this is sport.' The England coach, who had been taken to task not long before, with his talk of 'traitors' as he protested against the media treatment being meted out to his players over the Hong Kong and Cathay Pacific business, could not have been more right on this occasion as he spoke about the semi-final, against Germany. Once again, you feared that before it was all over, Euro '96 might well have become a dirty word, so far as England's participation was concerned. The scene was set for a battle royal between two old adversaries – you just hoped that the worst didn't happen.

This was the background ... 1966, and a World Cup final won 4-2 by England, after extra time; 1970, and a World Cup quarter-final won 3-2 by Germany after extra time; 1972, and a European Nations Cup quarter-final won 3-1 by Germany; 1982, and a 0-0 draw between England and Germany in their World Cup match during phase two of the finals in Spain; 1990, and a 1-1 draw in a World Cup semi-final ... followed by a 4-3, penalty shoot-out victory for Germany, after misses by Stuart Pearce and Chris Waddle. Now it was 1996, and England versus Germany at Wembley was a sell-out.

Venables was sweating on the fitness of Gascoigne, Adams, Sheringham and Anderton, and he had to replace the suspended Gary Neville; Germany's coach, Berti Vogts, had to wrestle with injury problems involving Jurgen Klinsmann and Fredi Bobic, having already lost Jurgen Kohler and Mario Basler. So there were anxieties for both team bosses, as they prepared their players for this penultimate encounter. Not surprisingly, the other semi-final between France and the Czech Republic was being regarded almost as a minor event ... although, should England survive against the Germans, Venables' team must meet one or the other in the final duel of all.

By the time the players walked out at Wembley, it was known that the winners would be meeting the Czechs – and that, after a guessing game about his presence or absence, Klinsmann was not among those about to line up for Germany. Yet the skipper did strive to exert an influence in one respect ... he had appealed for calm from his team's supporters, despite the intimidatory publicity. Klinsmann: 'The team can easily shrug off this sort of thing when it is time to play the match... I hope our fans will remain calm and that it won't spoil the atmosphere of this great occasion.' Among the near-76,000 crowd were some 7,000 German fans – and they were stunned when, inside three minutes, a bullet-like header from Shearer, via Gascoigne's corner and a flick-on from Adams, was buried in the German net.

Some 15 minutes on, and Germany had drawn level, as Moller and Helmer broke through and, as the ball crossed behind England's back line, Kuntz delivered a right-footer from 10 yards, to beat Seaman. From then on there were thrills and spills, near-misses and narrow escapes as each side did its utmost to gain supremacy ... but after 90 minutes it was still stalemate, and during extra time no-one could score the so-called Golden Goal. Not that it never looked likely, because Anderton's shot rebounded off the woodwork, with 'keeper Kopke a beaten man; Seaman was called upon to make a fine save from Moller; and from a corner, Kuntz steered home a header which, he believed, had brought him a second goal – until the referee, always in command, signalled that there had been a push.

Twice Gascoigne was not far short of getting on the end of crosses which evaded the German 'keeper, and you wondered if the England man was finally running out of steam, even though he was staying the course; and at the other end, Ziege went close to settling it before the time came for a penalty shoot-out. We all knew the score on that one ... it would be Shearer, Platt, Pearce and Gascoigne in turn, as it had been against Spain. The question was, could they do the business again – and would Seaman become a penalty-save hero the second time around? – One by one, the spot-kicks went in, with Hassler, Strunz, Reuter and Ziege replying for Germany.

So Sheringham stepped up to take penalty No.5, and he succeeded ... just as Kuntz did, when his turn arrived.

The moment of truth had also arrived – the moment when the footballing fate of a nation rested on the shoulders of the next man in ... Gareth Southgate. A player who, at the start of the tournament, might have considered himself somewhat fortunate to be thrust into the fray, because the odds would have been against this but for England's injury list. Southgate, however, had blossomed as the games went by, demonstrating through each one that he could more than measure up to the demands of football at the highest level. But in those few seconds as he drove the spot-kick goalwards, his world was to come crashing down – because Kopke leaped to his right, and made the save. So it was left to Germany's captain, Andy Moller, to settle the issue; and he made no mistake.

Southgate seemed devastated, no matter that Terry Venables and the player's team-mates offered him heartfelt consolation; yet no-one could deny that in a match where there had been so many willing to give their all, the Germans had been thoroughly tested ... and come through to show that they would neither lose their nerve nor buckle. After Kopke had made the fateful save, the cameras caught Venables – a man facing up to defeat as he slowly closed his eyes and registered the agony of someone who senses he is on a loser. The moment belonged to Moller and his German team-mates.

It was reported that the streets of England were deserted as millions watched the teams fight out 'a match which built to a finale of almost unbearable tension'. There had to be a sting in the tail, of course... 'However, a night of heroism turned to violence when English fans went on the rampage following the result. Vandalism and fighting with police continued into the early hours.' It was, seemingly, back to business as usual.

Business as usual? – As Terry Venables walked away into the sunset, amid talk of offers from Turkey, Pompey and Paris St. Germain, it was reported that 'the future of English football was yesterday placed in the hands of a Southampton coroner who promptly declared that he had never dealt with such a healthy body.' No, it wasn't Glenn Hoddle taking up a new occupation ... it was the vice-chairman of Southampton Football Club, Keith Wiseman (a solicitor), who had been 'the surprise winner of a four-cornered fight to succeed Sir Bert Millichip as FA chairman.' And once again the media – some of it , any way – had got it wrong ... because only 24 hours previously, it had been reported that of the four candidates for the top job in the Football Association, Geoff Thompson had strengthened his position as front-runner, Dave Richards had beaten off Wiseman's initial challenge by winning the backing of 18 of the country's top 20 clubs as the official Premier League nominee, and that Old Etonian Sir David Hill-Wood, was, like Wiseman, rated unlikely to get the nod when the FA Council met at London' s Royal Garden hotel to decide who should

Glenn Hoddle, the new England manager, taking a training session before the World Cup Qualifying game against Moldova

take the game into the 21st century.

It was mid-July, the excitement of Euro '96 was becoming merely a memory. And as the FA councillors prepared to get together, they all knew how it would work – the candidates polling fewest votes would be eliminated at each stage, so that finally it would be a head-to-head contest between the two most popular figures. These, it was said, were expected to be Geoff Thompson and Dave Richards. What happened was that Hill-Wood finished last in the first vote, Richards was eliminated in the second ballot, and hot-favourite Thompson lost to Wiseman – standing as an independent candidate – by 47 votes to 36. Wiseman's reaction: 'I think the FA has to hold the balance between the big clubs and the grass roots...' He also declared: 'After the success of Euro '96, I think the mood of the players and the country is as buoyant as it could possibly be. I could not imagine a better time to be taking over from Sir Bert. Euro '96 showed we can stage the largest and most complex of tournaments; it is very important that we now look ahead to hosting the World Cup in 2006. Bringing that tournament here will be a massive exercise, one that will occupy a great deal of my attention.' Well, we would all have to wait and see.

Meanwhile, Glenn Hoddle kicked off England's bid to reach the finals of the 1998 World Cup by steering his side to a 3-0 victory in Moldova, and to a hard-won, 2-1 success against Poland at Wembley. And on the October day when England were scraping their victory over Poland, two other protagonists were each claiming a victory, as Terry Venables and Alan Sugar finally settled their long-running libel battle. Venables was said to be 'jubilant', after Mr. Justice French had rules that his former employer was liable for costs (believed to be around £400,000) incurred since the ex-England coach had made a settlement offer in March ... while Sugar claimed to have been the winner after the judge had awarded him £100,000 Venables had already paid into court and ordered all unsold copies of Venables' autobiography to be pulped. Venables agreed not to repeat any of the claims in his book which had given rise to the action, and a High Court statement, it was reported, would formally bring this case to a close.

A few days later came news to boost England's hopes of staging the World Cup in 2006 ... it was reported that Euro '96 had made a record profit of £69 million.